DATE DUE

Oct 3rd	

WORLD
HISTORY SERIES ■ ■ ■

Maya
Civilization

Titles in the World History series

WORLD HISTORY SERIES

Maya Civilization

by
Patricia D. Netzley

LUCENT BOOKS
SAN DIEGO, CALIFORNIA

THOMSON
™
GALE

Detroit • New York • San Diego • San Francisco
Boston • New Haven, Conn. • Waterville, Maine
London • Munich

Library of Congress Cataloging-in-Publication Data

Netzley, Patricia D.
    Maya civilization / by Patricia D. Netzley.
        p.   cm.—(World history series)
    Includes bibliographical references and index.
    Summary: Examines the religion, art, architecture, society,
and intellectual pursuits of the ancient Maya, based on artifacts gathered at their ruins.
    ISBN 1-56006-806-X (hardback : alk. paper)
    1. Mayas—Antiquities—Juvenile literature. 2. Mayas—Social
life and customs—Juvenile literature. 3. Mexico—Antiquities—
Juvenile literature. 4. Central America—Antiquities—Juvenile
literature. [1. Mayas—Antiquities. 2. Mayas—Social life and customs. 3. Indians of Central America—Antiquities. 4. Indians of
Central America—Social life and customs. 5. Central America—
Antiquities.] I. Title. II. Series.
    F1435 .N39 2002
    972'.01—dc21

2001006271

Contents

Foreword

Each year on the first day of school, nearly every history teacher faces the task of explaining why his or her students should study history. One logical answer to this question is that exploring what happened in our past explains how the things we often take for granted—our customs, ideas, and institutions—came to be. As statesman and historian Winston Churchill put it, "Every nation or group of nations has its own tale to tell. Knowledge of the trials and struggles is necessary to all who would comprehend the problems, perils, challenges, and opportunities which confront us today." Thus, a study of history puts modern ideas and institutions in perspective. For example, though the founders of the United States were talented and creative thinkers, they clearly did not invent the concept of democracy. Instead, they adapted some democratic ideas that had originated in ancient Greece and with which the Romans, the British, and others had experimented. An exploration of these cultures, then, reveals their very real connection to us through institutions that continue to shape our daily lives.

Another reason often given for studying history is the idea that lessons exist in the past from which contemporary societies can benefit and learn. This idea, although controversial, has always been an intriguing one for historians. Those who agree that society can benefit from the past often quote philosopher George Santayana's famous statement, "Those who cannot remember the past are condemned to repeat it." Historians who subscribe to Santayana's philosophy believe that, for example, studying the events that led up to the major world wars or other significant historical events would allow society to chart a different and more favorable course in the future.

Just as difficult as convincing students of the importance of studying history is the search for useful and interesting supplementary materials that present historical events in a context that can be easily understood. The volumes in Lucent Books' World History series attempt to present a broad, balanced, and penetrating view of the march of history. Ancient Egypt's important wars and rulers, for example, are presented against the rich and colorful backdrop of Egyptian religious, social, and cultural developments. The series engages the reader by enhancing historical events with these cultural contexts. For example, in *Ancient Greece*, the text covers the role of women in that society. Slavery is discussed in *The Roman Empire*, as well as how slaves earned their freedom. The numerous and varied aspects of everyday life in these and other societies are explored in each volume of the series. Additionally, the series covers the major political, cultural, and philosophical ideas as the torch of civilization is passed from ancient Mesopotamia and Egypt, through Greece, Rome, Medieval Europe, and other world cultures, to the modern day.

The material in the series is formatted in a thorough, precise, and organized manner. Each volume offers the reader a comprehensive and clearly written overview of an important historical event or period. The topic under discussion is placed in a broad, historical context. For example, *The Italian Renaissance* begins with a discussion of the High Middle Ages and the loss of central control that allowed certain Italian cities to develop artistically. The book ends by looking forward to the Reformation and interpreting the societal changes that grew out of the Renaissance. Thus, students are not only involved in a historical era, but also enveloped by the events leading up to that era and the events following it.

One important and unique feature in the World History series is the primary and secondary source quotations that richly supplement each volume. These quotes are useful in a number of ways. First, they allow students access to sources they would not normally be exposed to because of the difficulty and obscurity of the original source. The quotations range from interesting anecdotes to farsighted cultural perspectives and are drawn from historical witnesses both past and present. Second, the quotes demonstrate how and where historians themselves derive their information on the past as they strive to reach a consensus on historical events. Lastly, all of the quotes are footnoted, familiarizing students with the citation process and allowing them to verify quotes and/or look up the original source if the quote piques their interest.

Finally, the books in the World History series provide a detailed launching point for further research. Each book contains a bibliography specifically geared toward student research. A second, annotated bibliography introduces students to all the sources the author consulted when compiling the book. A chronology of important dates gives students an overview, at a glance, of the topic covered. Where applicable, a glossary of terms is included.

In short, the series is designed not only to acquaint readers with the basics of history, but also to make them aware that their lives are a part of an ongoing human saga. Perhaps then they will come to the same realization as famed historian Arnold Toynbee. In his monumental work, *A Study of History*, he wrote about becoming aware of history flowing through him in a mighty current, and of his own life "welling like a wave in the flow of this vast tide."

IMPORTANT DATES IN THE HISTORY OF THE MAYA CIVILIZATION

1000–400 B.C.
Middle Preclassic Period.

11,000 B.C.
Nomadic hunter-gatherers widespread through Mesoamerica.

| 11,000 B.C. | 7000 | 4000 | 2000 | 1500 | 400 B.C. |

1500–1000 B.C.
Early Preclassic Period.

4000 B.C.
First Maya settlements established on Pacific and Caribbean coasts.

7000 B.C.
First permanent villages established in Mesoamerica.

900–1200
Early Post–Classic Period; intermingling of Maya with Toltec and other Mexican cultures.

250–900
Classic Period, also known as the Golden Age of the Maya.

Heiroglyphics found at the ruins of Palenque.

| 400B.C. | 0 | 500A.D. | 1000 | 1500 | 1600 |

1200–1500
Late Post–Classic Period; succession of internal conflicts.

400 B.C.–250 A.D.
Late Preclassic Period.

1519–1546
Spanish Conquest.

Piecing Together a Civilization

In the sixteenth century Spanish explorers conquered Mesoamerica, a region that encompassed what is now most of Mexico and upper Central America, and began searching for the riches they had expected to find in the New World. By the eighteenth century they had exhausted all obvious sources of wealth and their thoughts turned to hidden treasure. Could the jungles of Mesoamerica be concealing ancient stashes of gold?

In 1786 a Spanish military officer, Captain Antonio del Rio, was sent by his government to search for treasure in the ruins of Palenque, an ancient city in what is now the state of Chiapas in southern Mexico. There he and seventy-nine Indian workers hacked at stone temples and other time-worn structures with pickaxes until, as the captain reported, "Ultimately there remained neither a window nor a doorway blocked up, a partition that was not thrown down, nor a room, corridor, court, tower, nor subterranean passage in which excavations were not effected from two to three yards in depth, for such was the object of my mission."[1]

UNKNOWN ORIGINS

When del Rio found no gold he—and his government—lost interest in Palenque. But when the story of his treasure hunt was published in London, England, in 1822 as part of a small book entitled *Description of the Ruins of an Ancient City, Discovered Near Palenque* by Henry Berthoud, other Europeans became interested in the ruins. These included British archaeologist John Lloyd Stephens and artist Frederick Catherwood, who in 1839 and 1842 visited Palenque and wrote about their experiences in four books featuring engraved drawings of the site.

Readers of their work speculated on the identity of the people who had built the ancient structures. Some suggested that the ancient Greeks or Romans might have built and then abandoned the city. Others thought that the ancient buildings were once part of the Garden of Eden, destroyed when God cast the first man and woman, Adam and Eve, from paradise. Few nineteenth-century Europeans believed that the people of Mesoamerica were capable of creating such impressive structures.

AN AWE-INSPIRING SIGHT

Even though they had been damaged by del Rio's pickaxes the ruins were still an awe-inspiring sight, as were other ruins explored by subsequent archaeologists. Archaeologist George E. Stuart, who visited a site discovered in 1966, reports:

> It is difficult to imagine the impact that the . . . [Palenque] ruins had upon those who saw them for the very first time. I came closest to that realization at the small ruin of Chicanná, near the geographical center of the Yucatán Peninsula. . . . I first saw the building [there] through the forest about a hundred feet away. Its three doorways opened upon sunlight, for the rooms behind had caved in. But not the front. The stone-and-stucco

The discovery of the ruins at Palenque was the beginning of the study of Maya civilization.

façade of the long structure imitated a gigantic monster face. Great eyes stared from above the central entrance, and huge stone teeth hung over the doorway—the mouth of the face. A rubble-covered porch with a few teeth poking up through the dark leaf mold formed his lower jaw.

It was not the intricacy or the ornateness of the incredible structure, as I recall, that touched my emotions so. Rather, it was the contrast of the man-made symmetry with the wild and random tangle of vegetation that had all but reclaimed it. Chicanná will always be with me.[2]

A COMPLEX SOCIETY

Archaeologists now know that the people who built these ruins in the midst of the jungle were the ancient Maya, ancestors of the roughly 7.5 million Maya or part-Maya Indians living in Mesoamerica today. The ancient Maya had a complex society that modern scholars now classify as a civilization. This designation means that the Maya people had many sophisticated skills. Scholar Peter Harrison explains:

Civilizations have been defined in different ways in various parts of the world and in a variety of schools of academic thought. . . . Gordon Childe [an expert on high civilizations] required the presence of monumental architecture, a writing system, and at least rudimentary science. The Maya fulfilled all these requirements. They built in stone, raising public monuments that rival those of ancient Egypt in energy expenditure, as well as design and quality of fine art. Some of their ceramics were so finely crafted it is astonishing to realize that they were made without benefit of the [potter's] wheel, and their painting at its best has been compared to Michelangelo. Knowledge of astronomy, time, and geometry equaled that produced by many high civilizations of the Old World. Perhaps, most important, the Maya possessed a written script by which they recorded their own history, albeit subject to the kinds of editing that characterize all historical accounts. In that sense, the Maya may now be admitted into the company of literate peoples.[3]

LOOKING FOR ANSWERS IN MAYA LITERATURE

Unfortunately for scholars most of the Maya's written records, or codices, were burned in 1549, roughly two decades after Spain took over their lands. This destruction was intentional: Bishop Diego de Landa had been unwilling to tolerate any traces of the Maya's pagan religion in his domain. The Spanish churchman later wrote about these materials, forever lost to their creators and to history:

These people also made use of certain characters or letters, with which they wrote in their books their ancient affairs and sciences, and with these and drawings and with certain signs in these drawings, they understood their affairs and made others understand them and taught them. We found a great number of books in these characters, and, as they contained nothing in which there was not to be seen superstition and lies of the devil, we burned them all, which they regretted to an amazing degree and which caused them affliction.[4]

The books Landa burned were not only an expression of the Maya's religious beliefs but also a source of valuable information about their history, medicine, astronomy, and mathematics. Despite the Bishop's claim to the contrary three of the dozens of Mayan codices somehow escaped the flames; without these documents scholars would know far less about the Mayan civilization. The first is known as the Dresden Codex because it is housed in a public library in Dresden, Germany. This work, which surfaced in Vienna, Austria, in 1739, was written in approximately A.D. 1000. It offers information on Maya astronomy and mathematics.

The second codex is the Tro-Cortesianus, discovered in 1850 in Spain. Its name honors the Spanish explorer Cortés, who conquered much of Mesoamerica, with the prefix "tro" (two) referring to the fact that scholars originally thought that the codex

was two separate documents. This was a logical assumption because it was found in two parts in two different places and times. The Tro-Cortesianus is an astrological record probably written around the time of the Spanish Conquest in the sixteenth century.

The third codex is the Codex Peresianus, so named because it is housed in Paris, France, in the Bibliothèque Nationale (National Library). Probably written shortly before the Spanish Conquest it was found in 1860 in a box of uncataloged library documents. The Codex Peresianus is a record of Maya gods and religious ceremonies.

Some archaeologists believe that there are more codices waiting to be found, perhaps in some private library. However, without more such works from ancient times scholars have had to rely on two other sources of information about the ancient Maya: oral tradition among modern Maya and accounts of Maya history and culture produced around the time of the Spanish Conquest.

Accounts dating from the Spanish Conquest fall into two categories: works produced by the conquered and works produced by the conquerors. In the first category are books written in secret by anonymous Maya priests attempting to preserve their culture. These include the 1593 work *Book of the Jaguar Priest*, which recounts the history of the Maya from approximately A.D. 176 to the late 1500s, and the *Popol-Vuh*, or "Collection of Writings," which features the legends, mythology, religious beliefs and history of two branches of the Maya, the Quichè and Kakchiquel Indians.

All works by sixteenth-century Maya portray their ancient counterparts in the best possible light. The same is true for oral histories about the ancient Maya, passed down by the ancestors of the Central and South American people who encountered the Spaniards. Conversely, books about Maya culture written by Spanish authors, including Bishop Landa, display prejudices against the Maya. Therefore there is still much that today's scholars do not know about the Maya civilization—including why it disappeared—and many archaeologists consider the best source of information about the ancient Maya to be the artifacts gathered at their ruins.

Chapter

1 The Origins of Maya Culture

The lands of the ancient Maya covered a vast area of Mesoamerica including what are now parts of the Mexican states of Tabasco and Chiapas, all of the Mexican states of Campeche, Yucatán, and Quintana Roo, all of Guatemala and Belize, and substantial portions of El Salvador and Honduras. The Maya's territory consequently encompassed mild coastlands, tropical lowlands with thick vegetation, and cool dry highlands, each with a diversity of plants, animals, and minerals. This diversity provided the Maya with many resources that they could trade with other societies and thereby enrich their culture not only with goods but with new ideas. Many scholars believe that this enrichment directly led to the development of the Maya civilization.

FROM NOMADIC TO SEDENTARY

Before Maya society developed, however, its people were nomadic hunter-gatherers wandering from place to place in search of food. The first human beings to arrive in Mesoamerica probably migrated from Asia between twenty and forty thousand years ago, crossing a land bridge to North America before traveling south to Central America and Mexico. By 11,000 B.C., these hunter-gatherers were widespread throughout Mesoamerica.

Sometime around 7000 B.C., they began a roughly ten-thousand-year process of becoming sedentary, establishing permanent villages, and developing agricultural skills. Modern scholars believe that this transition was vitally important to the development of Maya culture. As professor of anthropology Robert Sharer explains, "Permanent settlements and stable sources of food supported ever larger populations and became the twin foundations for all the civilizations of the Americas."[5]

THE ARCHAIC PERIOD

For the Maya the transition from nomadic to sedentary life took place from approximately 6000 to 1500 B.C. Archaeologists have various names for this and other periods of Maya history; however, the one most commonly used is the Maya Archaic Period. During this period the first Maya

Tuluum is one of the many Maya settlements along the Caribbean coast.

settlements were established on the Pacific and Caribbean coasts, at least as early as 4000 B.C. In these places the climate was mild and the ocean provided a steady supply of seafood. In addition most villages were situated near a source of fresh water, most typically a river or stream, and around these sources the soil was rich enough to encourage the development of agriculture.

In fact, seed evidence has led some scholars, including anthropologist Michael D. Coe, to believe that these early Maya villages were responsible for the first cultivations of maize (also called corn, but with a grainier texture and shorter ears than the modern North American variety). He explains:

> It was in Mexico . . . that the all important plant foods of Mesoamer-

ica—maize, beans, squashes, chili peppers, and many others—were first domesticated. It seems likely that the practice of plant cultivation must have reached the Maya area at some time during the Archaic Period. . . . [Even if the very first corn was not grown in Maya lands,] Guatemala (which is no larger than the state of Ohio) has more distinct varieties of maize than can be found in all the United States put together, which suggests that this must have been a very old center for the evolution of this plant under the tutelage of man. Quite probably all the uplands, from southern Mexico through Chiapas and highland Guatemala, were involved in the processes leading to the modern races of this most productive of food plants.[6]

AGRICULTURAL ACCOMPLISHMENTS

The agricultural accomplishments of the Maya are particularly impressive considering the region in which they lived. With such a wide variety of climates and terrain, they had to change their farming techniques according to location. Instead of trying to plant on slopes, for example, they would remove soil at different levels to make flat terraces. In swamp and riverbed areas they would add soil to create raised flat planting areas. In forests and jungles they would slash and burn trees and vegetation to make fields. They also became aware that the ashes left behind by such burnings would act as fertilizer and thereby increase their crop yields.

The ancient Maya grew only a few basic crops. These included cotton, which they spun and wove into clothing, beans, sweet potatoes, and several kinds of chilies and squashes. They also went out into the wild to obtain foods like vanilla beans, avocados, pears, guavas, melons, mulberries, and small birds, animals, and fish. Typical food animals included monkeys, deer, rabbits, tapirs, and armadillos. In addition, the Maya trapped, tamed, and then bred wild doves, turkeys, and dogs for eating, although they also used domesticated dogs as watchdogs and hunting partners.

The main food for all Maya, however, was always maize. They would dry it, remove it from the cob, soak it overnight in water and lime to remove its hull, and then grind it by hand on a metate, or grinding stone, to create maize flour. This flour could be mixed with water and spices to create a pasty dumpling which was then wrapped in leaves to keep moist and taken to the fields for lunch. Maize flour might also be mixed with water and sweetened with honey to make a gruel, called atole, or flattened and cooked on platters of clay to make a thin pancake-like food, which was eaten alone or wrapped around beans or other cooked foods. This food is known today by its Spanish name: tortilla.

THE FIRST PEOPLE

Maize was so important to the Maya that they believed the gods made the first people out of corn. The following legend is found in the collection of sacred Maya writings known as the Popol Vuh, *as edited and translated into English by Delia Goetz and Sylvanus G. Morley.*

"And thus they [the Forefathers, the Creators and Makers] found the food, and this was what went into the flesh of created man, the made man; this was his blood; of this the blood of man was made. So the corn entered [into the formation of man] by the work of the Forefathers. . . . After [grinding the corn] they began to talk about the creation and the making of our first mother and father; of yellow corn and of white corn they made their flesh; of corn meal dough they made the arms and legs of man. Only dough of corn meal went into the flesh of our first fathers, the four men, who were created."

EARLY HOUSING

Growing, preparing, and cooking foods were a main part of Maya life. Perhaps for this reason the first Maya worshipped deities related to agriculture. In addition, life in early Maya villages centered around agriculture, as it did for other Mesoamerican cultures in their early years of development. Later, as Maya society developed more complexity, some of these early villages were transformed into cities. Others, however, remained farming villages with simple ways.

Maya villages had single-roomed huts of wood or stone, typically built on low platforms of earth or stone. Their steeply pitched roofs were thatched with palms in the lowlands and grass in the highlands. A man's first hut was typically beside that of his father-in-law, because Maya men could not marry without pledging to work for their bride's family for a certain number of years. (The specific number of years was announced during the marriage ceremony, but it was rarely less than six or seven.) Once the term of service was over (unless the man failed to work, in which case the bride's family cast him out and he was considered divorced), the man might build a new hut elsewhere, usually larger than the first to accommodate a growing family. In some villages this larger hut was the man's first, because there he lived in his wife's parents' home until his term of service was over.

However, even a larger hut still had only one room, perhaps divided by a blanket or screen into kitchen and sleeping areas. The sleeping area was usually bare; woven mats were put out at night as beds. In some cases, however, the area had raised sleeping platforms made with wood and plant matter. The kitchen had a stone hearth in the center of the floor; its smoke would travel up through a hole in the roof or waft out the gap in the wall that served as an entryway. Sometimes a cloth or blanket was hung over the entrance, but there was no door.

LIFE IN AN AGRARIAN VILLAGE

Modern scholars do not know exactly how the Maya's first villages functioned, but they can make assumptions based on the practices of modern Maya. Linda Schele and David Freidel, two of the foremost experts on Maya culture, believe that Maya farmers of today run their households much as their ancient ancestors did. They say:

> The archaeological record from . . . ancient villagers, as well as the description of the Maya by their Spanish conquerors, biased though it was, speaks to us of a cultural heritage which still lives on in Maya farming communities today. Granted that much has changed in the intervening

Maya dwellings were typically single-room huts with steeply pitched, thatched roofs.

centuries, there is still a basic connection between the ancient Maya and their descendants, just as there is between the ancient Saxons and the modern British. By examining modern village life, we can recover at least a partial picture of what life in those ancient villages was like.[7]

From studying modern Maya, experts surmise that ancient Maya lived in family compounds with several houses around an open courtyard. There were household gardens in the open spaces between houses where root vegetables, beans, corn, and other foods were grown for convenience and to provide surplus for trade. Houses were occupied by related adults and their children and grandchildren because, according to Schele and Freidel, "such extended families provide the large number of people needed in farming, a labor-intensive way of life."[8]

In fact, so much labor was required that often an entire village would share in the labor of each person's fields. Alternatively a village would have communal fields, each family reaping the harvest from one set portion of it. Planting and harvesting these fields could require as many as twenty men because the ancient Maya had no beasts of burden. This meant that all farming tasks had to be done with manual labor. Forests were cleared away using stone axes until only stumps remained; tree trunks and branches were sometimes used as fences to keep wild animals away from the field. To plant seeds farmers would poke a dibbling stick—which had a point hardened in fire—into

the soil, making a hole four to five inches deep. By hand they would sprinkle several seeds of different types into each hole, hoping at least one would grow. Many seeds were lost to small animals or poor growing conditions.

Different agricultural tasks were traditionally performed at different times of the year. Tree felling typically took place from August to November, a time of light rains. While one field was being cleared another was growing crops, and in November it was time to begin harvesting them. Harvest season lasted from November through May, a time of little or no rains during which crops ripened at different times. May to August was a time of medium to heavy rains, so this was when seeds were planted.

THE EARLY AND MIDDLE PRECLASSIC PERIODS

Maya agricultural practices worked well, providing the Maya with so much food that their population grew rapidly during the Archaic Period. When coastal villages became crowded their residents began to migrate up rivers to various lowland and highland areas in the interior of Mesoamerica. This period of migration, generally known as the Early Preclassic Period, took place between approximately 1500 B.C. and 1000 B.C.

Archaeologists know far less about the Maya's first highland and lowland villages because these places were located in regions that were subsequently subject to volcanic eruptions and erosion. In other

Pictured are the Maya ruins at Antigua, Guatemala. During the Classic Period, Maya civilization flourished in Guatemala.

words, little or no evidence of these villages exists today. However, archaeologists have found pottery, tools, and other artifacts in these areas that were apparently created around 1000 B.C.

In contrast, the oldest remnants of highland Maya cities date from around 100 B.C., although there are carved monuments in Guatemala dating from around 400 to 200 B.C. The period between 1000 and 400 B.C. is generally known as the Middle Preclassic Period and between 400 B.C. and A.D. 250 the Late Preclassic Period. During these times villages throughout Maya lands gradually grew into independent city centers, and shortly thereafter the Classic Period, also called the Golden Age of the Maya, began. The period from approximately A.D. 250 to 900 was when the Maya civilization truly flourished, and the heart of Maya lands during this period was in the tropical rain forests of north Guatemala.

ASIAN INFLUENCES

Archaeologists and anthropologists have long debated why and how the Maya civilization began. The current prevailing

Evidence of Possible Asian Influence

Some scholars believe that the Maya's book-manufacturing process offers ample evidence that the Maya were somehow subjected to Asian influences. Paper for the Maya's ancient codices was made by mixing fibers from the *Agave americana* vegetable plant with glue from resin and then pounding them flat, whereupon both sides were coated with white lime. These pages were folded like an oriental fan to make a "screenfold" book with blocks of wood as covers. Instead of letters the Maya wrote their texts in complex graphic characters called hieroglyphics, using vegetable-dye paint. All of these bookmaking and writing techniques were present in China, Southeast Asia, and Indonesia long before the Maya started using them, although the Maya hieroglyphics are unique to Mesoamerica. Therefore Michael Coe says in his book *The Maya*, "It is not unreasonable to suppose that it was through the medium of such books, which are still in use by Indonesian people like the Batak, that an intellectual exchange took place [between the Maya and some group of people in Asia]." However, Coe continues, "This by no means implies that the Maya—or any other Mesoamerican civilization—were merely derivative from Old World prototypes. What it does suggest is that at a few times in their early history, the Maya may have been receptive to some important ideas originated in the Eastern Hemisphere."

theory is that the Maya got the idea to create their society—which included powerful independent kingdoms that supported various government and cultural activities, a rigid class structure based on kinship, and a complex system of religious beliefs—from some outsider. Some scholars such as Michael Coe have theorized that this outside influence might have come from Asia, even though no Asian artifacts have ever been found in Maya lands:

One of the most persistent theories [to account for the rise of Maya civilization] holds that the previously undistinguished Maya came under the influence of travelers from shores as distant as the China coast. . . . [This possibility cannot be] easily dismissed. Its most consistent proponent has been Professor David Kelley of the University of Calgary, who has long pointed out that within the twenty named days of [one of the

Maya calendars] . . . is a sequence of animals that can be matched in similar sequence within the lunar zodiacs of many East and Southeast-Asian civilizations. To Kelley, this resemblance is far too close to be merely coincidental. . . .

Even more extraordinary, as the historian of science Dr. Joseph Needham reminds us, Chinese astronomers of the Han Dynasty as well as the ancient Maya used exactly the same complex calculations to give warning about the likelihood of lunar and solar eclipses. These data would suggest that there was direct contact across the Pacific. As oriental seafaring was always on a far higher technological plane than anything ever known in the pre-Hispanic New World, it is possible that Asian intellectuals may have established some sort of contact with their Mesoamerican counterparts by the end of the Preclassic.[9]

THE OLMEC

Most archaeologists and anthropologists, though, believe that these astrological and astronomical ideas originated not in the East but in another part of Mesoamerica. The ancient Maya traded with several different cultures, and two of them in particular could have shared their more advanced ideas with the Maya. These were the Olmec, who lived in the lowlands of Mexico's Gulf Coast from approximately 1500 to 400 B.C., and the Oaxacans, who lived in a highland valley of southern Mexico, the Valley of Oaxaca, during roughly the same period.

Both of these groups disappeared long before the Spanish conquered Mesoamerica, and they left behind virtually no writings. Most information about them has consequently come secondhand through the oral tradition of other Mexican cultures like the Aztec. However, archaeologists have been able to find artifacts that tell a little about what these civilizations were like.

Among the most extensive evidence has come from excavations of Olmec cities, most notably San Lorenzo and La Venta. Both of these sites are located near what is now Veracruz, Mexico. Archaeologists believe that the Olmec civilization began in San Lorenzo, which is near a branch of the Coatzacoalcos River, because its sculptures date back as far as 1200 B.C. However, for some unknown reason the city was destroyed around 900 B.C., whereupon the center of Olmec activity apparently shifted to nearby La Venta.

Located on a raised area in the middle of swampland created by the Tonalá River, the remains of La Venta have yielded several large pyramids made of earth once covered with stucco, as well as numerous stone funeral chambers, altars, and monuments. Some of the pillars at the site were carved from a type of hard volcanic rock called basalt, transported from a location approximately eighty miles away. These rocks weighed twenty to fifty tons and were probably moved by men pulling them along the ground on rolling

Aztec Cities

When Spaniards arrived in Mesoamerica they found not only the Maya but the Aztec, who had also developed a great civilization. About their first glimpse of Aztec cities in the Valley of Mexico in 1519, a Spanish soldier named Bernal Díaz del Castillo, who served in the army of Hernán Cortés wrote in 1632. This excerpt is quoted by Robert Sharer in Daily Life in Maya Civilization.

"When we saw so many cities and villages built in the water and other great towns on dry land and the straight and level causeway going towards Mexico, we were amazed and said that it was like the enchantments they tell of in the legend of Amadis, (with) the great towers . . . and buildings rising from the water . . . all built of masonry. And some of our soldiers even asked whether the things we saw were not a dream. . . . I do not know how to describe it seeing things as we did that had never been heard of or seen before, not even dreamed about."

logs. Such remnants of the Olmec civilization are similar to those left behind by the Maya.

An Influential Culture

More importantly, excavations at La Venta have made it clear that the Olmec were a forceful people capable of influencing the Maya and other Mesoamericans. Michael Coe explains: "From the unity of art style, from the size and beauty of the sculpted monuments, and from the massive scale of the public architecture, there can be no doubt that there was a powerful Olmec state on the Gulf Coast which even at this early time was able to command enormous re-

sources both in manpower and materials."[10]

The Olmec civilization was a chiefdom with a complex political structure, various social and religious constraints, and a succession of strong rulers. Each of these rulers in turn oversaw all trade as well as all agricultural activities, and they received a significant portion of their people's goods and crops for their own use, whether to eat or to trade. In addition they were responsible for their society's religious obligations, personally conducting rituals in honor of deities that included a fierce jaguar god and a toothed serpent god—two images that would later figure in Maya art. Carvings depicting these deities suggest that Olmec rituals were performed not only to thank the gods but to ensure good fortune, whether in the form of abundant crops, an easy labor during childbirth, improved health, or some other desirable occurrence.

Being in charge of all agricultural, economic, and religious aspects of Olmec life solidified the Olmec rulers' power and increased their wealth. They flaunted their supreme position in society through status symbols such as jade-covered scepters, and in death they were always buried with these possessions—again, a practice the Maya would later follow. During their lifetimes they were honored with upright rectangular stone monuments known as stelae featuring their portraits. As professor Robert Sharer explains, in these carvings archaeologists see some of the best evidence that the Olmec influenced the Maya.

> The motifs carved on Olmec monuments relate to themes seen on later Maya monuments—for example, a portrait of a ruler seated in a monster mouth, symbolizing a cave at the entrance to the underworld. Some Olmec rulers are identified by emblems that indicate either name or titles. We know that portraits of Maya rulers are identified by hieroglyphs of their names and titles. After a ruler's death, both the Olmec and Maya followed the custom of defacing or breaking that ruler's monuments, probably to cancel the supernatural power [they believed to be] within the stone.[11]

The Maya and Olmec cultures shared other traits as well. Like the Maya, the Olmec had a calendar and a knowledge of astronomy and mathematics. Their temple architecture and monuments were also similar. In addition both groups played games featuring hard balls made of rubber from local trees. Consequently many modern scholars are convinced that the Maya copied the Olmec ways, although the Maya were still primitives during the period when the Olmec civilization was flourishing. Pamela Francis offers an example in her book *What Became of the Mayas?*:

> For a long time the two groups [the Olmec and the Maya] must have lived side by side, visiting and perhaps trading or warring with each other, but when the Olmecs were carving their colossal baby-faced statues the Mayas still lived in villages of primitive huts, and when the Mayas began to build their great pyramids the glory of the Olmecs had already faded into memory.[12]

THE OAXACAN

Other scholars, however, believe that the Maya were influenced not by the Olmec but by the Oaxacans. Toward the end of the Middle Preclassic Period (which lasted from approximately 1000 to 400 B.C.), the Olmec civilization had begun to break apart, apparently because of political disputes and other problems within their society. Meanwhile, the Oaxacan civilization was reaching its peak of power and glory.

Pictured is a stone carving of a two-headed serpent. Olmec and Oxacan influence can be seen in Maya culture by their worship of serpent gods.

As with the Olmec, the Oaxacans developed agriculture, had a calendar, built temples, and worshipped jaguar and serpent gods. They also erected monuments to their rulers. However, these monuments featured portraits not only of the rulers themselves but also of their slaves and their sacrificial victims. Such images appear in some Maya artwork as well. In both cultures the images were apparently used as symbols of power.

Both cultures also had a rigid class structure based on social and economic differences, and many elements within this structure were the same. Therefore some archaeologists believe that the Maya could have received inspiration for their own civilization through contact with the Oaxacans, or perhaps through contact with some other culture that traded with the Oaxacans. In either case, some also believe that the Oaxacans were likely influenced by the Olmec. For example, Michael Coe says:

> Whether or not one thinks of the Olmec as the "mother culture" of Mesoamerica, the fact is that many

other civilizations, including the Maya, were ultimately dependent on Olmec achievement. This is especially true during the Middle Preclassic [Period], when lesser peasant cultures away from the Gulf Coast were acquiring traits which had filtered to them from their more advanced neighbors, just as in ancient Europe barbarian peoples in the west and north eventually had the benefits of the achievements of the contemporaneous Bronze Age civilizations of the Near East.[13]

A Vast Trading Network

Most archaeologists have concluded that trade was the means by which the early Maya learned how to grow their crops, honor their gods, and structure their society. Most further believe that there was once a vast trading network with central marketplaces scattered throughout the region, and that the Maya were integral to this network. For example, Sylvanus G.

Morley and George W. Brainerd, two of the foremost experts on the ancient Maya, report that

> Although no conclusive physical evidence of ancient markets [actual locations where trading took place] exists, these trade centers were noted at the time of the Conquest, and their antiquity is assumed. But direct archaeological evidence for ancient trade in a variety of commodities does exist [in the form of minerals, bird feathers, and other items found where they would not occur naturally]. . . . The ancient Maya were a crucial part of a system of long-distance trade routes that ran the length and breadth of Mesoamerica and beyond. The Maya occupied an area intermediate between Mexico and Central America and rich in highly desirable resources. . . . These assets established them as essential middlemen.[14]

In other words, the Maya were drawn into the Mesoamerican trading network not only because of their central location in the region but because they had many goods that other people wanted. These included agricultural products, obsidian and flint for weapons and tools, salt, cotton, cacao (chocolate), macaw and other bird feathers for headdresses, amber, jade, pyrite for mirrors, bark paper, coral, and jaguar pelts and teeth. Such items were transported over land by traders who carried their goods on their backs; canoes were used to carry things down rivers and, toward the end of the Maya civilization, over oceans as well.

Once the Maya became a part of the Mesoamerican trade network their society grew increasingly complex, developing many of the characteristics that eventually helped their civilization achieve greatness. In particular, according to Morley and Brainerd, trading practices were responsible for creating class distinctions within Maya society, thereby giving the upper classes the power necessary to build a great civilization:

> The development of centralized markets was undoubtedly a crucial factor in the growth of Maya society. Because goods could be exchanged in a single centralized location, a village could engage in specialized production (of textiles or pottery, according to its environmental potential), take its products to the market center, and exchange them for other necessities from other villages. The result was an economic unity and interdependency focused on the market center, and each such market was linked to others by means of long-distance trade, as well. . . . Together, these economic factors were a powerful stimulus for social organization and development. The marketing centers, to which the villages were tied, were controlled by the emerging elite class, and the resulting economic power accorded the elites became a crucial foundation for their status and authority. Those centers in locations favorable to acquiring essential goods or controlling important

trade routes . . . developed the organizations necessary to strengthen the control of the acquisition, transport, and distribution of trade goods. As the managers of these organizations, the elite increased their wealth, prestige, and power.[15]

Trade, then, not only gave the Maya ideas about how their society should be established but also provided the means by which this establishment could occur. By the end of the Middle Preclassic Period (around 400 B.C.), the Maya's participation in the Mesoamerican trading network had changed their economy, altered their political system, and created a class structure that impacted every aspect of their culture.

Chapter

2 Maya Society

During the Middle Preclassic Period (1000 to 400 B.C.) the Maya developed societies known as chiefdoms. Beginning in northeast Guatemala, these societies grew in power and sophistication throughout the Late Preclassic Period (400 to 250 B.C.), and by the Classic Period—the Golden Age of the Maya—all had achieved the level of complexity characteristic of a state. This accomplishment was due to changing notions regarding the role and status of the individual within society. As a result, status eventually became one of the most important elements of Maya society, evident in every aspect of daily life.

PRECLASSIC CHIEFDOMS

Once the Maya became a part of the Mesoamerican trading network, each village needed some kind of central authority to oversee the activities of merchants. Chiefdoms were the answer to this need. In primitive societies a chiefdom is led by a chief or headman whose power derives from supernatural and economic sources. In most cases a wealthy man is named chief because his people believe that his

wealth is derived from his having special access to the gods. Once he becomes chief his wealth increases still further because his people pay him to ask the gods to bring them good fortune.

Because the role of chief is a lucrative one, individual chiefs typically passed the job on to their sons, arguing that their lineage carries a superior ability to communicate with deities. However, the power of a chief can disappear if a natural disaster or other unfortunate event causes the villagers to stop believing that he has a strong standing with the gods. There are no government, social, or religious institutions dedicated to supporting a chief's rule, no strong military to keep him in his position of power.

DEVELOPING MAYA STATES

In contrast, a state (also called a polity or kingdom) is a political entity ruled by a central authority, usually a king, whose power is reinforced by a network of government, social, and religious institutions. These include a hierarchy of military and political officials dedicated to maintaining the status quo. States are therefore far more complex than chiefdoms, and often they develop from chiefdoms whose societies have become stratified, or layered, with many levels of power.

Those at the top of such a society want to maintain their positions, and so they create a physical and mental environment that protects their interests. To do this they not only establish institutions that cement their power but also promote ideas that encourage citizens to want a monarchy. Specifically, those in power convince the populace that having a king will improve the lot of every member of society and that the king deserves his lofty position because of the benefits he can offer his people.

In the case of the Maya, the people came to believe so strongly that kings were superior to chiefs that some deliberately converted their chiefdoms to kingdoms rather than allow this evolution to take place gradually. Linda Schele and David Freidel, who have spent years studying ancient Maya culture, describe what must have happened in the village of Cerros around 50 B.C. when its people made this transition:

> The people of Cerros . . . consciously [decided] to embrace kingship as an institution and the consequences of that decision were profound for all. In the space of two generations, this small fishing village transformed itself into a mighty acropolis. Every living soul in Cerros participated in that transformation, from the lowliest fishermen and farmers who provided food for the laborers, to the most

gifted stonemasons who carved the building facades, to the shamans who gave the temples their blessing. It is difficult for us to imagine such complete and rapid social metamorphosis.[16]

MAINTAINING THE ORDER OF SOCIETY

The Maya eventually became convinced that although chiefs and kings both ruled because they could petition the gods for favors, only a king had the support of the gods. Because of this support the gods would punish any person who failed to obey and serve a king. This punishment might be an accident, an illness, or a death, either to the individual or a family member. Alternatively the gods might take out their anger on all of Maya society by ending the rain or starting a war. Only by maintaining the order of society would the Maya be ensured prosperity. According to Schele and Freidel,

> The . . . magical person of the king was the pivot and pinnacle of a pyramid of people, the summit of a ranking of families that extended out to incorporate everyone in the kingdom—from highest to lowest. . . . The farmer, the stonemason, and the craftsperson might pay tribute to the king, but the king compensated them for their service by giving them a richer, more enjoyable, more cohesive existence. The people reaped the spiritual benefits of

This figurine depicts a Maya king. The Maya saw their king as an intermediary between themselves and the gods.

the king's intercession with the supernatural world and shared in the material wealth his successful performance brought to the community.[17]

CREATING A HIERARCHY

The king ensured that the order of society would be maintained by surrounding himself with trusted subordinates. Many of these subordinates were relatives of the king, and they included priests as well as government and military leaders. Sylvanus G. Morley and and George W. Brainerd elaborate:

In the case of the ancient Maya, there is some evidence that rulership was claimed as a kind of divine right . . .

TIKAL

One of the greatest Maya cities was Tikal. In his book The Maya, *archaeologist Michael Coe reports on the discovery of its ruins and their current state.*

"It is more than likely that the ruins of Tikal, in the very heart of the Petén [area of Guatemala], were first encountered by the brave Father Avendaño and his companions in 1695. Lost and starving among the swampy *bajos* [lowlands] and thorny forests of northern Guatemala, they came across a 'variety of old buildings, excepting some in which I recognized apartments, and though they were very high and my strength was little, I climbed up them (though with trouble).' Tikal, now partly restored by the University of Pennsylvania, is a giant among Maya centers; it is the largest Classic site in the Maya area, and one of the greatest in the New World. Particularly impressive are its six temple-pyramids, veritable skyscrapers among buildings of their class. From the level of the plaza floor to the top of its roof comb, Temple IV, the mightiest of all, measures 229 ft (70 m) in height. The core of Tikal must be its great plaza, flanked on west and east by two of these temple-pyramids, and on the north by the acropolis . . . with its Late Preclassic and Early Classic tombs. Some of the major architectural groups are connected to the Great Plaza and with each other by broad causeways, over which many splendid processions must have passed in the days of Tikal's glory. The 'palaces' [which archaeologists can only guess were royal residences] are also impressive, their plastered rooms often still retaining in their vaults the sapodilla-wood spanner beams which had only a decorative function."

[but while] there was a single office for the highest political authority in each major center, . . . a measure of power may have been delegated to other officials with specific functions. These offices were probably held by members of the ruling lineage, brothers, sons, and other relatives of the ruler. . . . [There is also evidence] that power was shared by the leaders of several elite lineages, although one "royal" lineage seems to have furnished a single supreme ruler in most instances.[18]

More importantly, the hierarchical nature of the state promoted the idea that every member of society was essential to its well-being, thereby further strengthening public support for a kingship. Schele and Freidel explain that

The farmer offering a gourd bowl of water and white corn gruel to the spirits of his field was less knowledgeable about the intricacies of royal symbolism and religion than the king who, standing in one of the great plazas of his city, offered his blood in a painted clay plate to the ancestors of all Maya. Yet the farmer knew that

Pictured is a statue of a priest of Chac, the god of rain. Priests played an important role in Maya society.

what he did was essentially the same. . . . The king and the farmer inhabited the same world. Even though they understood . . . [aspects of] that world on different levels, their lives in it were dynamically interconnected. The successful performance of the king as the state [priest] . . . enriched the farmer's life in spiritual and ceremonial ways. His performance in economic affairs brought wealth to his kingdom and gave his constituents access to goods from far places. Royal celebrations and rituals generated festivals that touched all parts of the community emotionally and materially. The great public works commissioned by the kings created the spaces in which these festivals and rituals took on meaning.[19]

CLASS STRUCTURE

The king and the farmer were members of the two main Maya social classes: the elite and the nonelite. Members of the elite class were wealthy while those of the nonelite class were not. Within the elite class there were two groups, one with much higher status than the other. In the former group were members of the royal lineage. In the latter were priests, merchants, professional warriors, and people with large holdings of land.

Most members of the nonelite class were farmers. Of these the majority farmed their own small tracts of land, usually within a village's communal field. Others worked the fields of elite landowners. Also in the nonelite class were unskilled laborers and skilled craftsmen (although some of the more sophisticated artisans came from the elite class). Skilled craftsmen were of higher status than either the laborers or the farmers.

MARRIAGE

Status within each social class determined not only what job a person could hold but also whom that person could marry. A woman's father selected her future husband when she was just a girl, choosing from suitors whose interest in the marriage was expressed through a professional matchmaker. The matchmaker would bring a gift on behalf of some young man to the girl's parents, and if they accepted it then the marriage plans could proceed. The actual ceremony, however, would not take place until the girl was around eighteen to twenty years old; before then she continued to live with her parents and was forbidden to speak to any of the unmarried men in her village. Meanwhile unmarried young men lived in a communal hut, although they still received meals from their parents.

Men from the nonelite class typically had only one wife, while those from the elite class might have several. For either class divorce was an easy affair, accomplished simply by mutual consent. A man or woman who sought to marry a second time, whether after divorce or death of a spouse, could choose a new partner without going through parents or matchmaker, and no wedding ceremony need be performed.

Wedding ceremonies among both the elite and nonelite were typically conducted by a shaman, not a priest. The reason for this had to do with the fact that marriage was a personal matter with relatively no impact on society as a whole. Priests, who were of the elite class, were concerned with religious matters related to the gods' support of the state, performing ceremonies, divinations, and other duties believed to benefit a large number of people. In contrast, shamans, who were of the nonelite class, were responsible for matters related to the personal lives of the Maya—healings, divinations related to the fortunes of individuals and their village, and ceremonies related to birth, puberty, marriage, and death. Some of these required the services of *chacs,* assistant shamans who helped prepare participants for the ceremony.

DAILY WORK

Elite and nonelite children both went through the same basic ceremonies, but otherwise their experiences differed. Nonelite boys were trained to perform tasks related to agriculture, hunting, fishing, and toolmaking, while nonelite girls were trained to prepare food, weave clothes, make domestic pottery, and run the household. Meanwhile, elite boys were trained to become priests, warriors, merchants, government officials, artisans, or scribes. Elite women sometimes partic-

ipated in duties related to religious rituals; in fact, on a few occasions a woman ruled when there was no male heir to the kingdom or until the male heir came of age. For the most part, however, elite women did little because they had nonelite women as servants.

In addition to servants—nonelite men and women who voluntarily served the elite—the Maya enslaved one another. There were three ways for a Maya to become a slave. First, the head of a household might sell one of its members into slavery to alleviate the poverty of his family. Second, the state might decree that someone who committed a crime become a slave. Third, a person from one state who had been captured by another during a war automatically became a slave, unless the captive was a member of the elite class. In this case the person was typically killed as part of a ritual offering to the gods.

STATUS AND APPEARANCE

Another difference between the elite and nonelite was in how the two groups dressed. Women of both classes wore embroidered cotton garments, either a blouse and skirt or a loose dress, but the style of the embroidered design differed according to the person's social standing and village. Priests, who were always male, also wore dresses, but theirs were far more elaborate than any woman's. Other men of both classes wore two cotton garments: a loincloth, called an *ex,* and a square shawl, called a *pati,* the latter of which

THE HETZMEK

The ancient Maya valued children and would ask the gods—particularly Ix Chel, the goddess of childbirth—to send them many. Once each child was born, the gods would provide the parents with its paal kaba, *or given name, during a ceremony with a shaman; this name was used along with the father's family name, the mother's family name, and the child's nickname. A short time later the child went through another ceremony to become a part of Maya society. Robert Sharer, in his book* Daily Life in Maya Civilization, *reports that such a ceremony is still performed by Maya today, although his description suggests that it might have been influenced by the Christian concept of godparents.*

"The Maya still perform ceremonies marking a child's acceptance into society. In Yucatan this ceremony is the *hetzmek*, performed when the baby is carried astride the mother's hip for the first time. For girls the hetzmek is held at three months; for boys, at four months. The girl's age of three months symbolizes the three stones of the Maya hearth, an important focus of a woman's life. The boy's age of four months symbolizes the four sides of the maize field, the important focus of a man's life. Participants in the ceremony, besides the infant, are the parents and another husband and wife who act as sponsors. The child is given nine objects symbolic of his or her life and is carried on the hip nine times by both sponsoring parents. The ceremony closes with offerings and a ritual feast."

was also used as a blanket. However, the *ex* and *pati* of the nonelite men were plain while those of the elite were elaborately colored, patterned, and decorated with feathers. The same disparity in appearance was true for the men's sandals, which had a sole of deer hide and were tied to the feet with thongs. The nonelite wore plain sandals with a simple method of tying, while the elite wore decorated ones with elaborate ties. Kings also wore headdresses covered with feathers of the quetzal bird, which was considered sacred, as well as cotton capes covered with feathers and/or jaguar pelts, the latter always considered a mark of high rank. Sometimes instead of a headdress the king would wear a decorated headband.

Warriors going into battle also wore headdresses and carried banners as well. Modern scholars disagree on what weapons they carried; some say the most common weapon was the bow and arrow while others say the warriors only carried spears and slingshots. Still others believe that all three of these weapons were common, as were swords with handles of wood and blades of obsidian. Shields were framed with sticks and covered with jaguar or deerskin. In addition some warriors wore a padded cotton garment that covered the entire body as armor.

Warriors typically burned their hair at the crown of their heads to make themselves bald there. While recovering from this dangerous and painful procedure, they grew the remaining hair long and wound it in a band around the head. Other men as well as women also wore their hair long, perhaps tied up on the head, but did not burn it. The heads of the elite also looked different from those of

Maya warriors adorned themselves with headdresses covered with feathers, as this painting from the fifth century shows.

the nonelite. Elite infants had their heads bound between two boards, one across the forehead and another across the back. The bones of a child's skull are initially soft and can be molded into whatever shape they are forced into as they harden. When this hardening process was complete the Maya removed the boards and the child was left with a forehead that would always be flat—yet another mark of elite status.

Still another clue to a woman's status was her jewelry. Nonelite women wore plain bone, wood, stone, pottery, or shell earrings as well as simple nose and lip jewelry. Elite women wore earrings and nose and lip jewelry of jade, obsidian, or coral. Additional decorations worn only by the elite include ankle bands, necklaces, bracelets, and other decorative items. Many featured intricate mosaics. Men sometimes wore jewelry as well and, like the women's, their decorations also indicated their status. Kings wore a great deal of jade because it was associated with the gods. Kings and the elite also drilled holes in their front teeth and decorated them with inlays of jade, obsidian,

A flat forehead was considered a mark of elite status among the Maya. To achieve this, Maya infants had their heads bound between two boards.

or iron pyrites. A cosmetic practice that developed over time was the filing of teeth to points. All Maya filed at least some of their teeth to a point, believing them to be more beautiful this way.

Men also announced their status through the use of body paint, with different colors representing different social positions. Warriors, for example, used black and red while priests were painted blue. (This color was also painted on sacrificial victims right before they were killed because at that moment they were as connected to religious rites as priests were.) Colored tattoos, which could be put on both men and women any time after marriage, served a similar function. These were on the face as well as the body. Bishop Landa described the tattooing process he witnessed:

> The more they do this [tattooing], the more brave and valiant they are considered, as tattooing is accompanied by great suffering, and is done in this way. Those who do the work first paint the part which they wish with color and afterwards they delicately cut in the paintings, and so with the blood and coloring matter the marks remained in the body. This work is done a little at a time on account of the extreme pain.[20]

OTHER MARKS OF STATUS

The elites' homes were in or near the city, and although their houses were essentially the same as the nonelite they were better constructed. In most cases,

the nonelite did not have stucco on their walls because of the added expense, while the elite always did. Burial practices also separated the elite from the nonelite. The former were buried under temple and palace rooms, or in city plazas that had been dug up to receive their stone coffins, called sarcophagi. The final resting place of the nonelite was usually the dirt beneath their homes. Generally, the more prestigious the location, the more important the deceased. In addition the elite were buried with helpers—not only animals but also nonelite servants that had been sacrificed upon the death of their master—as well as with valuable jewelry, pottery, and other objects befitting their status.

During their lifetimes the activities of the elite also indicated their status. For example, they had the money and leisure time to hold many banquets. Archaeologist Dr. Thomas Gann describes what he believes these events were like:

> The banquets were frequently very costly affairs, the host spending in the entertainment of his guests a small fortune. The guests sat at small low tables for two or four persons. After the conclusion of the meal the guests were served cups of honey wine until they were intoxicated. The wives of the guests [who were always all male] waited outside to conduct their drunken husbands home. . . . [Nevertheless] numerous fights and brawls occurred, the men sometimes even burning down their own houses in their drunken frenzy.[21]

PUBERTY CEREMONY

In ancient times all Maya children went through a puberty ceremony to mark their entrance into adulthood. As part of the ceremony two symbols of childhood were removed. For a girl this symbol was a red shell that had been tied around her waist when she was four years old; for a boy it was a small white bead that had been fastened to his hair around the age of three. In his book Daily Life in Maya Civilization, *Robert Sharer reports on what this ceremony was like at the time of the Spanish Conquest and suggests that it was the same in ancient times.*

"In colonial Yucatan [a Maya calendar] was consulted to select an auspicious day for the community puberty ceremony marking the end of childhood and the beginning of adulthood. It was held every few years for all children deemed ready to take this step. The ceremony was conducted by a shaman; four assistant shamans, or *chacs* (after the Maya rain god); and a respected elder man of the community. . . . After the chacs placed pieces of white cloth on the children's heads the shaman said a prayer for the children and gave a bone to the elder, who used it to tap each child nine times on the forehead. The shaman used a scepter decorated with rattlesnake rattles to anoint the children with sacred water, after which he removed the white cloths from their heads. The children then presented offerings of feathers and cacao beans to the chacs. The shaman cut the white beads from the boys' hair, and the mothers removed the red shells from their daughters' waists. Pipes of tobacco were smoked, and a ritual feast of food and drink closed the ceremony."

MAYA CITIES

Although some archaeologists believe that both elite and nonelite lived in the city, others think that the only nonelite to live in the city were servants of the elite. The majority, however, think that the function of the cities was not primarily residential. Elizabeth P. Benson, an expert in pre-Columbian civilizations, claims that:

Maya cities in the Central area were probably not true cities. They were sacred centers used on ceremonial occasions and for markets, both of which must have been frequent in the Maya world. Perhaps a small, select population lived in them permanently, but the archaeological remains do not yet give evidence of any sizable permanent population. The populace lived outside the centers and came in only for special events. Maya cities vary greatly in size and importance. Smaller sites were surely purely ceremonial, but perhaps it may some day be proven that a site like Tikal was actually a city. In the Highland area Kaminaljuyú was a large ceremonial and residential center as far back as Middle Pre-Classic times, and in the Yucatán area, in the Post-Classic period, Mayapán was a residential city.[22]

However, all Maya undoubtedly had to visit the city in order to petition government officials for help with various problems. Consequently residential areas, whether for nonelite or for both elite and nonelite, grew up just outside of various cities, and as their populations grew, the line between the city center and its surrounding suburbs blurred. This was surely the case in the city of Tikal, the "Place of Voices," which Dr. Thomas Gann calls "the largest, and perhaps the most important of all Maya cities."[23] The center of Tikal was roughly one square mile, its suburban residential area two to three square miles. Gann reports that "The unit in laying out the city [of Tikal] was the quadrangular plaza, round which

Glyphs cover the walls of a temple in Tikal, the most important of all Maya cities.

were clustered the temple and dwellings of the priests. These were added to, century by century, till the city reached gigantic proportions, connoting a very large population, probably a quarter of a million or more."[24]

CITY HIERARCHIES

Not all cities, however, were as prestigious as Tikal. Just as there were levels of status among the Maya people, so too were there different levels of status among Maya kings and their cities. A king's prestige was dependent upon the wealth of his state, and his level of authority was determined by how much good fortune his state experienced. Whenever some disaster occurred—such as a drought or heavy losses in war—the king was blamed for not keeping the gods happy. Once a king appeared to have lost the favor of the gods, rival kings in other kingdoms were emboldened to attack him. If this attack was successful, the vanquished king was usually killed (if he hadn't already died in battle) and his kingdom was taken over by the victor.

Through warfare certain states expanded their territory to include a cluster of city centers with their surrounding villages. One city in this cluster would be designated the capital, and the others would be considered its subordinates. Each of these cities had a different level of prestige; as with the Maya people, their cities' places in the hierarchy were determined by wealth. However, if the king of a large state became weak, some of the subordinate cities might try to break away, led by another member of the royal lineage. In this way, new kings and new states were created.

The first cities were located in the highlands and on the coastal plains of Maya territory, where the Maya civilization apparently reached its peak far earlier than in the lowlands (Late Preclassic as opposed to Early and Middle Classic). The largest and seemingly most prestigious of the highland cities was Kaminaljuyú, or "Place of the Ancient Ones," which covered approximately three square miles in the Valley of Guatemala. It began as a trading center and grew into a center for all political, economic, and religious activities in the region. As such, it had temples, large plazas for ceremonial activities, monuments, shrines, tombs, market centers, and a network of canals to carry water throughout the city.

Tikal was among the most prestigious lowland cities along with Uaxactun. Uaxactun and Tikal are about eleven miles apart in northeast Guatemala, and some archaeologists believe that they were the first and second cities, respectively, to be established by the Maya. Dr. Thomas Gann, who led an expedition to several Maya ruins in the 1890s, describes the central ruins at Uaxactun:

> What may be termed the Capitol, at Uaxactun, was built on the summit of a small hill, apparently artificially flattened for the purpose. It contained the temples, plazas, open courts, and commemorative stelae,

with the private residents of the rulers and chief priests connected with the temple worship. The whole is now in a more or less ruinous condition, and not one building remains intact. From the top of this Capitol a magnificent view is obtained of the surrounding country, which in the days of the city's greatness was doubtless covered with the thatched wooden houses of the poorer people, beyond which extended in all directions a green ring of growing maize, the main support of the people.[25]

The construction of Uaxactun was a good beginning for the Maya; eventually there were over 100 great Maya cities, although some were abandoned as others were built. These included not only Uaxactun and Tikal but also Copán, Tuluum, Palenque, and Chichén-Itzá, founded at various periods in Maya history. Together they remain the best representation of the Maya's religion, art, architecture, and society.

3 Maya Ideology

Religion was a unifying element of society. All social classes from the king and lesser elites to the peasantry shared the same beliefs, which were supported by the state. Therefore although trade provided the Maya with the means to establish their civilization, religion was the true foundation on which it was based. As anthropologists Linda Schele and David Freidel explain:

> The principal language of our reality here in the West is economics. Important issues in our lives, such as progress and social justice, war and peace, and the hope for prosperity and security, are expressed in material metaphors. Struggles, both moral and military, between the haves and have-nots of our world pervade our public media and our thoughts of the future. The Maya codified their shared model of reality through religion and ritual rather than economics. The language of Maya religion explained the place of human beings in nature, the workings of the sacred world, and the mysteries of life and death, just as our religion still does for us in special circumstances like

marriages and funerals. But their religious system also encompassed practical matters of political and economic power, such as how the ordered world of the community worked.[26]

COMPLEX BELIEFS

The Maya's view of reality is difficult for Western minds to understand. Essentially the Maya believed that there were two dimensions: the Otherworld, which was for the gods, and the human world. These two dimensions existed among three realms: the heavens or Upper World, which was the home of celestial gods, the earth or Middle World, which was the home of the Maya, and the Underworld, also known as Xibalba, which was the home of the underworld gods and the spirits of the human deceased. The celestial realm had thirteen layers and the underworld realm nine layers, each ruled by one god but populated by others. In other words, the realms of the gods had the same kind of hierarchical system and sense of order as the realm of humans.

The Maya had an equally complex view of the earth's position in reality and the gods' relationship to this position. Anthropologist Michael D. Coe offers this explanation, one of several different expert opinions on a topic about which scholars have little direct information:

> Maya cosmology is by no means simple to reconstruct from our very uneven data, but apparently they conceived of the earth as flat and four-cornered, each angle at a cardinal point which had a color value: red for east, white for north, black for west, and yellow for south, with green at the center. The sky was multi-tiered, and supported at the corners by four Bacabs, Atlantean gods with the appropriate color associations. Alternatively, the sky was held up by four trees of different colors and species, with the green ceiba or silk-cotton tree at the center.[27]

The Underworld

Modern scholars also disagree on the nature of the Maya's Underworld. The Spanish who conquered the Maya wrote that their view of an afterlife involved an Underworld with various places where

Pictured in this detail is a Maya god of the Underworld, just one of the many deities worshiped by the Maya.

the deceased would dwell forever, either in happiness or suffering. In other words, the Maya Underworld shared with the Christian afterlife the concepts of heaven and hell where good people are rewarded and evil people are eternally tormented. For this reason some experts suspect that, intentionally or unintentionally, Spanish reports of the Maya afterlife reflect the beliefs of their European authors. Others disagree, arguing that Spanish reports of the Maya afterlife accurately reflect Maya beliefs.

There are disagreements as well about the meaning of various aspects of Maya burials in terms of the Maya's religion. For example, in excavating tombs in the city of Tikal, Dr. Peter Harrison found something strange in one tomb:

> The most fascinating features of this burial are in two large ceramic vessels placed one over the head and one over the loins of the main figure. The bowl over the head region contained the cramped skeletal remains of an adult female, while the bowl over his loins held the remains of an infant under a year of age. Who these [individuals] might have been raises a plethora of speculations. Could they be his wife and child, cramped into vessels to accompany him in his tomb?[28]

Harrison encountered other mysteries in Tikal's tombs as well. About the tomb of a king he reports:

> [The ruler] had been dismembered following death. His skull and thigh

bones were not included in the burial. We now know that these important parts of the body were occasionally omitted from a royal burial. . . . It is a matter of speculation just why specific parts of the human body were sometimes retained and not included in a burial. Was it a matter of parts missing in action, lost in war, or retained by the enemy as trophies? Or was this the result of familial retention of these parts for much the same reason? Reverence of the dead, and even for specific body parts of the dead is clearly indicated, whether or not this reverence came from enemies or friends.[29]

MAYA DEITIES

Archaeologists are also uncertain about the validity of their assumptions regarding many Maya gods, who were no less complex than the Maya view of reality. The Maya believed that the gods could change their nature as well as the form in which they appeared to humans, which means that the same god might be depicted in many different ways in ancient artwork. This has made it difficult for archaeologists to identify individual gods and to connect each one to all its forms. Michael Coe explains:

> Exceedingly little is known about the Maya pantheon [their set of recognized gods]. That their [Otherworld] was peopled with a bewildering number of gods can be seen in the eighteenth-

New Year Ritual

Because of the Maya's obsession with time the coming of the new year was very important to them. In her book The Maya World, *Elizabeth Benson, who has studied the writings of the Spanish conqueror Bishop Diego de Landa and has observed modern Maya rituals as well, offers this description of Maya New Year festivities past and present.*

"According to Bishop Landa, each town in Yucatán had two facing piles of stones at each of the four entrances of the town, which marked the four world directions, or cardinal points. At the time of the New Year ceremonies the image of the new god, with the appropriate color, was placed on the heap facing the image of the god who had ruled for the previous four years. There were then various rituals and processions, and the image of the god was censed with copal resin ground with maize. A bird was sacrificed by decapitation, and the idol was then placed on a frame representing one of the world-direction trees. This was followed by other processions, dances, and rituals. In the twentieth century, in the area where the Year-Bearer's ceremony is still celebrated, a period of [sexual] abstinence is observed by those participating in the ceremonies. A chicken or turkey—the choice depends on the wealth of the participants—is decapitated, tree branches are cut and tied to a cross, and beeswax candles are burned in front of the church door. The ceremony has become inextricably merged with Christian symbols, but its roots are firmly planted in the Maya past."

century manuscript, "Ritual of the Bacabs," in which 166 deities are mentioned by name, or in the pre-Conquest codices where more than thirty can be distinguished. This . . . multiplicity results in part from the gods having many aspects. Firstly, each was not only one but four individuals, separately assigned to the color-directions [red/east, white/north, black/west, and yellow/south]. Secondly, a number seem to have had a counterpart of the opposite sex as consort. . . . And lastly, every astronomical god had an underworld avatar [a deity in bodily form], as he died and passed beneath the earth to reappear once more in the heavens.[30]

Archaeologists theorize, however, that the most important god of the Maya was Itzamna, or "Lizard House." He had two other forms, Hunab K'u, which means "first living god," and Kukulcan, "feathered serpent." The Maya apparently believed that he also manifested himself in the heavens as the Milky Way. Itzamna created all existence including writing and human knowledge, controlled all aspects of life and death in all realms, and supervised all other gods.

Two other important gods were Kinich Ahau and Hunahpu, the sun god and the god of the planet Venus, a very bright star visible to the naked eye in Mesoamerica. The sun god had many forms, just as the sun appears to have many forms as it passes from dawn to dusk. These forms include a young man (dawn), a dying man (dusk), and a jaguar (night). The sun god was believed to be in the Underworld at night, and the Venus god was thought to coax him out of that realm every morning, since Venus typically appears right before dawn.

Of particular significance to farmers were Yum Kax, the god of fertility and maize, and Chac, the rain god, who was often depicted as a reptilian creature with snake-like fangs. There were four variations of the rain god, each associated with a different color and direction: red for the Chac of the east, black for the Chac of the west, white for the Chac of the north, and yellow for the Chac of the south. The four men who typically assisted the priests were called chacs in honor of these variations.

Other members of society also had gods with a special interest in their well-being. Gods associated with merchants, for example, include Ah Chicum Ek, god of the North Star, who led merchants home from faraway places, and Ek Chuah, who was the god of traders and cacao, a main trading crop. A god important to women was Ix Chel, or "She of the Rainbow," who was responsible for childbirth, healing, and divination. Gods associated with death and disease include Yum Cimil, who carried away the sick and dying to the Underworld; Buluc Chabtan, a god of war and human sacrifice; and Ixtab, a god of suicide (which was not considered to be a wrongful act).

The Maya also believed that every person had a spirit companion who could influence that person's life. These spirits dwelled with the gods in the Otherworld—specifically in that part called the Underworld—but humans could communicate with them through prayers and rituals and at certain locations. Caves in particular were thought to be sacred places where the spirits of the dead could be contacted.

NOURISHING THE GODS

The gods, however, could be present anywhere. Although the three realms were typically depicted as being one atop the other, the Maya actually understood them as intertwined rather than as separate planes. Schele and Freidel explain:

> These two planes of existence were inextricably locked together. The actions and interactions of Otherworld beings influenced the fate of this world, bringing disease or health, disaster or victory, life or death, prosperity or misfortune into the lives of

A statue of Chac, the Maya rain god, stands in front of a temple at the Maya ruins in Chichén-Itzá.

human beings. But the denizens of the Otherworld were also dependent upon the deeds of the living for their continued well-being. Only the living could provide the nourishment required by both the inhabitants of the Otherworld and the souls who would be reborn there. . . . To the Maya, the . . . kings were, above all, divine shamans who operated in both di-

mensions and through the power of their ritual performance kept both in balance, thus bringing prosperity to their domains.[31]

The kings' nourishment of Otherworld beings was made possible by the central tree, also called the *wacah chan*, which had its roots in the Underworld, its trunk in the Middle World, and its branches in the Upper World. Touching all levels of existence, this tree acted as a conduit between the two worlds. Through ritual, the king could move its location to the place where he was standing, then open a doorway into the Otherworld. At this moment, he was able to feed the gods with food offerings or blood. The Maya believed that blood was the container for every living being's sacred essence (called the *kul* or *chul*, depending on the region) and thought that the gods grew stronger and happier by partaking of it.

BLOODLETTING AND SACRIFICES

A reflection of Maya beliefs about the sacred nature of blood was a practice called bloodletting, the cutting (but not necessarily killing) of a person or animal to release blood. Bloodletting was a part of many Maya rituals, with the source of the blood dependent upon the desired outcome of the ritual. Small requests of the gods needed only small birds and animals while big requests or major events called for large animals. For example, seventeen jaguars were sacrificed in a rit-

CENOTE SACRIFICIAL VICTIMS

For many years after the Spanish Conquest stories abounded about the sacrificial victims thrown into cenotes. These victims were said to be beautiful girls and were typically portrayed as romantic heroines, but as Michael Coe reports in his book The Maya, *archaeological evidence suggests that most of the victims were men and children and that their deaths were anything but romantic.*

"Shortly before the Spanish Conquest, one of our colonial sources tells us that the victims were 'Indian women belonging to each of the lords,' but in the popular imagination the notion has taken hold that only lovely young virgins were tossed down to the Rain God lurking below its greenish-black waters. The late Dr. Hooton, who examined a collection of some fifty skeletons fished up from the Sacred Cenote [at Chichén Itzá], commented that 'all of the individuals involved (or rather immersed) may have been virgins, but the osteological evidence [evidence obtained from skeletal remains] does not permit a determination of this nice point.' A goodly number of the skulls turned out to be from adult males, and many from children, while pathology showed that 'three of the ladies who fell or were pushed into the Cenote had received, at some previous time, good bangs on various parts of the head . . . and one female had suffered a fracture of the nose!'"

This Maya sculpture depicts a human sacrifice to the sun god. Human sacrifice was one way that the Maya appeased their gods.

ual to dedicate a temple altar in the city of Copán.

Rituals performed to appease the gods sometimes required a king to cut himself in order to provide blood for the ritual. Maya art also shows blood being drawn from the tongue or other body parts of the elite for various rituals, particularly ones related to fertility. The most common way to draw human blood, however, was through a ritualistic sacrifice. In such a sacrifice the victim was usually a war captive, a slave, or the child of parents who believed that the death of their offspring would bring good fortune to the rest of their family.

The Maya sacrificed their victims in several ways. One way was to slit the victims' throats; another was to disembowel them. In the city of Chichén-Itzá in the Yucatán, sacrificial victims were cast into a cenote, which was a natural well created when the earth caved in over a subterranean lake or river (a common phenomenon in the Yucatán). There were actually two cenotes in Chichén-Itzá, one supplying the city's drinking water and the other a place for victims to be sacrificed in order to appease the gods of rain. The latter, called the Well of Sacrifice or Sacred Cenote, is approximately 150 feet in diameter; the surface of the water is a distance of 60 feet down and the water's depth about another 60 feet. About this cenote Bishop Landa wrote: "Into this well they have had, and then had, the custom of throwing men alive as a sacrifice to the gods in times of drought, and they believed that they did not die though they never saw them again. They also threw into it a great many other things, like precious stones and things which they prized."[32]

A more common method of human sacrifice used in many other Mayan cities involved stripping the victims naked, painting them blue, and taking them to a sacrificial altar just outside a temple. There each victim was held down while a priest cut open his or her chest to pull out a still-beating heart. The heart's blood was then smeared or splashed on an idol of the god who was the focus of the ritual. Other blood was dried for later use as incense, as the Maya believed its smoke could carry their requests to the gods during prayers and rituals.

THE HERO TWINS

Human sacrifices were typically conducted as part of rituals related to maintaining the order of society and the balance of the two dimensions and three realms. These include rituals to bring rain, increase the bounty of crops, and dedicate temples and ball courts. In fact, events related to ball courts were the most common reason that human sacrifices were conducted. The reason for this lies in a myth related to ball playing.

In this myth, which is recounted in the *Popol Vuh*, two expert ballplayers—twin brothers Hunahpu and Xbalanque, also known as the Hero Twins—were taken to the Underworld to play ball against the Lords of Xibalba, the gods of death. Jealous of the humans' skills, the gods attempted to torture them and steal their playing gear; the twins cleverly escaped but eventually died in a fire. Shortly thereafter they came back to life, disguised themselves, and returned to the Underworld to exact revenge. Having retained the ability to become whole again after death, they then amazed the residents of Xibalba with this skill. According to the *Popol Vuh:*

> They [Hunahpu and Xbalanque] cut themselves into bits; they killed each other, the first one whom they had killed stretched out as though he were dead, and instantly the other brought him back to life. Those of Xibalba looked on in amazement at all they did. . . . Presently the word of their . . . [ability to reform] came to the ears of the lords [of Xibalba]. . . .

The lords were astounded. "Sacrifice yourselves now, let us see it! . . ." said the lords. "Very well, Sirs," they answered. And they proceeded to sacrifice each other. Hunahpú was sacrificed by Xbalanqué; one by one his arms and his legs were sliced off; his head was cut from his body and carried away; his heart was torn from his breast and thrown onto the grass. All the Lords of Xibalba were fascinated. . . . [Hunahpú] returned to life. . . . "Do the same with us! Sacrifice us!" they [the lords] said. "Cut us into pieces, one by one!" . . . And so it happened that they [sacrificed the lords] . . . and they did not bring either of them back to life.[33]

In this way, the Hero Twins—who were subsequently transformed into the gods Kinich Ahau (the sun god) and Hunahpu (the Venus god) and went to live in the heavens—succeeded in exacting revenge on the gods of death by killing them and refusing to heal them. But according to Professor Robert Sharer the Maya were more concerned with the rebirth aspect of the tale than with its message of revenge. He explains by stating the Maya beliefs about the Hero Twins legend:

> The rebirth of the Hero Twins after being sacrificed is a metaphor for human rebirth after death, a theme celebrated by the Maya ritual of human sacrifice. The ball court was the setting for the confrontation between the Hero Twins from this world and the death gods of Xibalba. In many Maya cities, the ball court symbolized the

DRUG USE

The Maya apparently used drugs as part of their religious ceremonies. In his book Daily Life in Maya Civilization *Professor Robert Sharer reports on their type and usage.*

"The ancient Maya . . . used a variety of substances that altered the individual's normal state of consciousness as part of divinatory ritual. The taking of narcotics, hallucinogens, and other psychotropic substances by shamans was seen as a way to transform themselves and communicate with the supernatural realm. Experiences in these altered states were understood as messages from the gods that could be interpreted to answer questions and determined future events. Some active substances— especially alcohol and tobacco—were consumed by the general populace, but most of the more potent hallucinogens and psychotropic agents were reserved for specialists and for ritual divination."

threshold between the earthly realm and Xibalba. The ritualized ball game played in this arena re-enacted the original confrontation between the Hero Twins and the death gods. Maya kings had the closest associations with the Hero Twins. Kings had the power to enter Xibalba and confront the death gods, play the sacred ball game, and perform human sacrifice. When a Maya king was captured by another in war, he was taken to the ball court to be defeated and sacrificed by decapitation. Thus he was sent to Xibalba to be born again in the sky in a ritual that re-enacted the myth of the Hero Twins.[34]

BALL COURTS

Because this reenactment had such a profound meaning in terms of the Maya's religion, they developed strong feelings regarding the ball game the Hero Twins had played, and they connected this game to various religious rituals. In fact, in some places religious cults apparently sprung up among devotees of the game. This apparently occurred in Chichén-Itzá, for example, which had a total of seven ball courts; other cities had as many as 15 ball courts. In most places animals were sacrificed before and after each game in addition to the humans sacrificed to dedicate a new playing court, so temples were usually built adjacent to these facilities. Archaeologist Dr. Peter D. Harrison, who studied the ruins of the Maya city of Tikal from the late 1950s through the 1960s, described the ball courts there:

> The few ballcourts known from Tikal vary more in scale than in form. The most obvious ballcourt today is the small group in the Great Plaza just south of Temple I. . . . The axis of this court aligns with a building high above in the Central Acropolis, and the northern room of this structure likely served as a royal viewing stand. . . . The other most prominent examples are found in the Plaza of the Seven Temples where three playing courts spread across the entire north side of the plaza. . . . From the north side, the Plaza of the Seven Temples could be entered only by passing through one of the playing fields of the three parallel ballcourts. . . . The playing courts are all oriented north-south. Sloping side benches were used in the game to bounce the ball back into the playing field. . . . Adjacent at a higher level were platforms accessible by stairs where viewers could watch the game. The court in the East Plaza showed evidence that these viewing platforms were covered. Our only evidence for the specific type of game played is in the form of displaced carved monuments that could easily have served as ballcourt markers.[35]

From the artwork depicted on such monuments, archaeologists believe that the game played on these ball courts was Tlaxtli, which still existed at the time of the Spanish Conquest. Played by two

Hitting markers like the one shown here was the goal of the Maya game of Tlaxtli.

teams of two to eleven men each, this game required each team to score points by hitting a hard rubber ball at or through a particular goal; in Central Maya cities this goal was a marker or a particular section of the court, while in outlying cities like Chichén-Itzá it was one of two rings set high at the midpoint of the ball court's two side walls. In hitting the ball through these rings, the player could not use his hands or feet, but only another body part such as a hip or elbow. Players wore extensive padding to make sure the hard ball, which was roughly two to ten inches in diameter and about five pounds in weight, would not bruise them. Scoring a goal through a ring was so difficult that during many such games no points were scored; and if a goal finally was

Pictured is the pyramid of Kukulkan, a Maya pyramid from the eleventh century A.D. located at Chichén Itzá.

made, the spectators were obliged to give the scoring player their jewelry and/or their clothes. For this reason many spectators ran away the minute a goal was scored, or they removed all of their jewelry prior to a game.

After such an event or any other public religious ritual the assembled crowd participated in various celebrations that included drinking, music, and dancing. Men and women usually danced separately. Musical instruments included several kinds of drums and rattles as well as clay or wood flutes and whistles. Music was also a part of the religious ceremonies themselves, played at various moments in the ceremony and accompanying move-

ments of the priests. Rituals related to divination often involved hallucinogenic drugs as well as music.

EVER-PRESENT SIGNS

In addition to large public rituals the Maya performed various private rituals as they went about their daily lives. For example, they made food offerings before eating and said prayers before farming. The gods were a part of every aspect of their existence and therefore always on their minds.

The gods were even apparent in the structure of Maya cities. Buildings generally were oriented according to both their purpose and their relationship to the Otherworld. For example, palaces were in the center of the city because the king who lived there was the center of the Middle World, which in turn was at the center of the three realms. Ball courts were oriented north-south because they were associated with the Otherworld; north was the direction associated with the celestial realm and south with the Underworld. Similarly, tombs of kings were usually located north of the palace, because kings were believed to go to the celestial realm as gods, rather than to the Underworld as spirits, after they died.

The artwork on these structures and others also reflected their religious associations. Consequently any Maya walking through the city would have been reminded of the gods at every turn. However, although scholars have suggested various meanings for buildings and artwork, experts remain uncertain about the conclusions they have drawn.

4 Art and Architecture

The Maya expressed their beliefs regarding their gods and their society through both art and architecture. To this end, they produced numerous buildings, sculptures, carvings, pottery vessels, figurines, and other objects. This is fortunate for modern scholars because without these remnants from ancient times they would know far less about the Maya civilization.

PLANNING A CITY

The most obvious fact discovered through Maya ruins is that the Maya were accomplished builders for their time, creating cities that were extremely elaborate. For example, the city of Tikal included five pyramids with temples at their summits; numerous residences; and seven building complexes with as many as forty-two buildings each, including palaces and administration buildings as well as raised stone roads and stone water reservoirs. Moreover, these structures might represent only a fraction of what the city once was. Dr. Peter Harrison, who conducted excavations in Tikal in the 1960s, explains:

By the time of its collapse in the 10th century, Tikal covered roughly 65 sq. km, with over 3,000 known surface structures. As many as 10,000 ruined buildings and platforms may lie below the surface. The population reached a figure of somewhere between 100,000 and 200,000, although arguments are entertained for even greater numbers.[36]

In most cases cities developed over time, so archaeologists find various layers of new buildings atop old as well as individual buildings that display evidence of remodeling. Elizabeth Benson explains how this worked:

Most of the pyramids and temples were not built at one time. Throughout the Maya area it was customary to build a newer and larger pyramid over the old one, so that the old one became a core with the skin of the new pyramid wrapped around it. Instead of tearing the old structure down completely, Maya builders covered it up with a new building. In many sites, archaeologists have left the sightseer a glimpse of the previous construction, or constructions, within the new one.[37]

Sometimes, however, entire cities were mapped out and constructed at once, usually near or on the ashes of villages destroyed to make way for the new structures. For example, in discussing the "urban renewal" program undertaken by the residents of Cerros in about 50 B.C., Linda Schele and David Freidel report that the people

> buried their [original] village completely under broad plastered plazas and massive temples. Families conducted sacrifices over the foundations of their old homes, acknowledging for one last time the ancestors who lay buried below the floors and patios. They then smashed the vessels for their leavetaking feast, broke jade jewelry with great rocks, and scattered the bits and pieces over the homes they would never see again. Finished with one way of life, they walked outward and began building new homes in a halo some 160 acres in breadth around the new center.[38]

MAYA CITIES

The writings of Bishop Diego de Landa offer a glimpse of the structure of ancient Maya cities. Elizabeth Benson quotes Landa in her book The Maya World.

"Before the Spaniards had conquered that country, the natives lived together in towns in a very civilized fashion. They kept the land well cleared and free from weeds, and planted very good trees. Their dwelling place was as follows: in the middle of the town were their temples with beautiful plazas, and all around the temples stood the houses of the lords and the priests, and then the most important people. Then came the houses that were richest and belonged to those who were held in the highest estimation nearest to these, and at the outskirts of the town were the houses of the lower class. And the wells, if there were but few of them, were near the houses of the lords; and they had their improved lands planted with trees for making wine and they sowed cotton, pepper, and maize, and they lived thus close together for fear of their enemies, who took them captive, and it was owing to the wars of the Spaniards that they scattered in the woods."

Before beginning work on any building Maya architects planned its construction with care, often in consultation with their king. Their primary goal appeared to be to create structures whose exteriors reflected the magnificence of their king and their gods. Consequently their buildings are much more elaborate on the outside than on the inside, and certain buildings—particularly temples—sit high in the landscape to call attention to that elaborateness. Architects also apparently made an attempt to achieve in their buildings the same balance and order valued in the workings of their society; as a result, their structures display a symmetry in

This modern drawing depicts the balance and order that Maya architects sought when designing their cities.

both shape and decoration. For example, if a particular decoration appeared on one side of a commemorative pillar, it would appear on the opposing side as well.

But although there were common elements among Maya buildings throughout the civilization, architects adopted slightly different styles of construction and decoration depending on their location. For example, whereas in the city of Tikal the temples had single doorways, in Palenque they had multiple doorways. In Copan the emphasis was on impressive stairways and elaborate mosaics on building exteriors. Cities that were subject to frequent attack featured additional walls as well as moats and other fortifications. Experts though they were in wall building, however, the Maya lacked one important architectural skill: the ability to build arches.

ARCHES

No Maya building had any doorways with a true arch because no Maya architect knew how to make one. At the peak of a true arch is a single stone called a keystone, which bears the full pressure of the arch; if the keystone were to be removed the arch would fall down. But the Maya had not discovered the keystone principle, so they used what are called false arches instead. A false arch lacks a keystone, therefore every one of its stones bears equal weight. Dr. Thomas Gann describes how the Maya built this type of arch and how it influenced a building's design:

The false or cantilever arch was constructed in the following manner. When the side walls of the building reached the desired height, usually six to twelve feet, their inner faces were brought together by means of overlapping courses, like two inverted stairways placed opposite each other. When only a small interval was left at the top this was covered over with flat flags of stone.

The disadvantage of this form of arch is that, unlike the true arch, where each stone is self-supporting, the weight of each course has to be carried by the one beneath it, in consequence of which a great mass of solid masonry is required in the walls of the building, to act as counterpoise to the outward thrust of the arch. A further disadvantage is that the breadth of the chamber is necessarily limited to the span of the arch, which with the masonry used by the Maya could never exceed eighteen feet. In buildings constructed along these lines the room space is about equalled, and in some cases considerably exceeded, by the solid masonry necessary to contain it.[39]

Architects in the city of Palenque, however, found a way to make the rooms of their temples bigger. Archaeologist Paul Gendrop of the University of Mexico, who studied the ancient ruins, explains:

The architects were true masters here [in the city of Palenque]. They discovered an important secret of construction. Instead of keeping the upper facades of the temples as vertical, they made them slant backward—at the same angle as the slant of the corbeled vaults [false arches] inside. This gave them a lighter structure, which allowed wider rooms and much larger doorways. At Tikal, many of the rooms are so narrow they hardly seem worth the trouble of building them; the walls are sometimes twice as thick as the rooms are wide. Here at Palenque, just the opposite is true.[40]

CONSTRUCTION MATERIALS

Regardless of the city or the type of construction Maya builders relied on one substance—limestone—for most of their work. The walls, floors, and ceilings of their large structures were all constructed of thick limestone blocks covered with plaster that was made by burning the limestone to create an ash of lime and wood and then mixing this ash with water.

Building foundations were made of white lime earth, built up in layers. Onto this earth the builders laid flat, hard

Maya builders relied exclusively on limestone for walls, floors, and ceilings of all their structures.

stones, then raised a broad platform with internal walls to create compartments they could fill with coarse broken limestone. Once completed this platform was topped with another layer of white lime earth. Into the earth they usually mixed pieces of pottery broken during a ritual to bring blessings on their building endeavors.

Some buildings were constructed atop only one platform. Others, particularly temples, were atop many. In fact, building floors might be anywhere from 2 to 180 feet off the ground. The platforms for temples were typically in the shape of a pyramid, a result obtained by stacking platforms of diminishing size to the desired height. This required the builder to make precise calculations to ensure that the final platform at the summit would support the intended structure.

At least one and perhaps all four sides of the pyramid beneath a temple had stairs leading up to the top. Archaeological evidence suggests that these stairs not only gave people access to the temple but were also an important part of religious expression. Kings would use the steps as a place to conduct public rituals, usually on a landing in the middle and/or the top of the stairway. The stairs leading to each landing as well as completely up the pyramid typically totaled a number considered sacred. For example, the pyramid temple in the city of Cerros had four stairs to the first landing and nine stairs to the summit threshold, both four and nine being sacred to the people who lived there.

Another important religious element of temple architecture was its exterior decorations. These might include large sculptured stone masks of the gods, plaster moldings, paintings, and mosaics. Colors were often chosen on the basis of their religious symbolism. For example, red—the color of East, the place where the sun rises each morning—symbolized the Sun God and rebirth. Black, on the other hand, was connected to death and the Underworld because it represents the absence of light.

The techniques involved with decorating a temple required a great deal of skill. Linda Schele and David Freidel, who visited the ruins of Cerros, relate their assumptions regarding how Maya artists decorated a temple there:

> The final work on this temple can only be described as a magnificent performance of consummate skill and cooperative effort. The panels of stone on the terraces of the pyramid base stood ready to be adorned with divine images. The artisans who applied the wet plaster and modeled the elaborate details of these four masks . . . had to work rapidly and surely. These artisans used a few previously prepared appliqué elements that could be stuck on with plaster glue, but for the most part they had to know what the final images would look like even before they started. It was vital to shape the plaster before it cured. Even with retardants added to the plaster, the sculptors had about thirty minutes in which to apply and work the material before it hardened under their hands. . . .

Maya temples were built by stacking platforms of diminishing size until the desired height was reached.

While the plaster was still damp, the painters began their work, adding red, pink, black, and yellow lines to highlight the natural color of the raw plaster and to render even finer details in the images. . . . To finish their work before the plaster dried, the artists had to work frantically, dripping and throwing paint with the force of their strokes. Yet even these drip patterns were incorporated as part of the imagery. The mastery of their craft is evident in the sureness of their drawing and the confidence of their swirling lines.[41]

The images on the base of the Cerros temple include a jaguar god and the Hero Twins. The temple also featured four carved tree trunks located at points representing each of the four directions. Schele and Freidel believe that these trunks were carved only after being anchored in four sockets in the temple floor, and that the king oversaw the raising of the trees during a special sanctification ceremony. They also believe that "Once the building was partially sanctified and activated, it had to be completed rapidly, for [the Maya believed that] the raw power within it was potent and needed the containment that only ritual use by the king could provide."[42]

Schele and Freidel further believe that this temple's rooms were constructed in order to allow the king to move from room to room in a counterclockwise direction, from east to west, when going from the building's innermost room to the outside where rituals were held. They suggest that this movement pattern was an attempt on the king's part to echo the movement of the sun from east to west. They call the innermost room "the heart of the temple, the place where the king carried out in solitude and darkness the most intimate phases of his personal bloodletting and the most terrifying phases of his communion with the Otherworld."[43] Their theories come from depictions of the king's actions in temple carvings.

STELAE

Many impressive carvings have been found in Maya ruins, not only on temple walls but also on wood or stone lintels

Platforms leading up to the Maya temples were often decorated with carvings and paintings.

(door frames), stone altars and sarcophagi, and stelae. These rectangular columns might be made from wood but were more commonly carved from large single slabs of stone. Some of these slabs weigh sixty-five tons and are as tall as thirty-five feet, although most are five to twelve feet tall.

Stelae were typically placed in front of important buildings in ceremonial centers during the Early, Middle, and Late Classic periods. Each one is marked with the date it was erected, as well as with other inscriptions and images. Archaeologist George Brainerd, an expert in stelae, reports:

> The subject matter of the stela carving is remarkably uniform in all areas and over the 550 year span documented by the carved dates. Nearly all stelae of the central Maya area are decorated with a single, elaborately costumed male figure carved in bas-relief [a type of sculpture where the figure stands out from the background]. This figure, either priest, ruler, or god, dominates the composition and his tremendous plume-bedecked headdress is often fitted closely to a border which frames the front face of the stela. Rectangular or L-shaped panels of glyphs [Maya hieroglyphic writing] included in the front panel gives dates or, presumably, descriptive material, and additional human figures, usually smaller than the main figure, appearing to be acolytes, slaves, or captives, are frequently shown. Additional decorative and glyphic pan-

els often were carved on the sides and, less often, on the back of the stela. Stelae were most frequently set on a low platform in a plaza at the foot of the central staircase ascending to a major temple. Additional stelae were added after the first, normally forming a row or cluster, at the ends of successive 20-year or even 5- or 10-year calendric periods.[44]

OTHER CARVINGS

The inscriptions on stelae apparently provide information about the lives of the people represented on them as well as dates that were important during those people's lifetimes. However, the number of stelae erected varied throughout Maya history from only a few in the late sixth century to dozens of them in A.D. 731.

Meanwhile the Maya produced many other kinds of stone carvings. In fact, one of the most impressive carved stones found in an excavation of Maya ruins was not a stela. When archaeologists were investigating a tomb in the city of Palenque in 1952 they discovered a slab that they thought was a stone altar, but when they raised it off the ground they saw the remains of a man underneath and realized that it was the lid of a sarcophagus. Archaeologist George Stuart describes this find:

> The huge carved slab, made of the fine yellowish-white limestone that the sculptors of Palenque reserved

for their most important works, was in pristine condition. Twelve by seven feet, it depicts the figure of a man reclining on the glaring face of an earth monster. Below it, and reaching up to embrace the figure, are great fleshless jaws. Behind and above the human figure rises a tree, doubtless the sacred ceiba. Atop it perches a huge bird.[45]

MURALS

Other forms of artwork also depict elements of the Maya religion. These include wall frescoes, mosaics, pottery vessels, and murals. Perhaps the most impressive Maya murals were found at Bonampak in Mexico, near its border with Guatemala. Discovered in 1946 by Mexicans searching for chicle to make chewing gum, these murals cover the walls of three rooms in a ruined building and feature realistic scenes of people engaged in various activities against a solid background. Elizabeth Benson offers this description of the Bonampak murals:

> The three rooms seem to tell a connected story, for some of the same characters appear in more than one scene. The scenes probably represent, first, preparations by dancers impersonating the gods of the earth, then a raid on a small settlement and the capturing and bringing back of prisoners, and finally a sacrificial ceremony and dance. Above the scenes are a series of masks and symbolic motifs. Paintings of scenes like these show objects used by the Maya—clothing, weapons, musical instruments, costumes of the dance, headdresses and ornaments of the nobles, etc. They depict methods of fighting and sacrifice. Because they show activities not normally recorded in sculpture, they give a glimpse into Maya ceremonial life.[46]

POTTERY

Painted pottery also provides images from Maya life. During the Classic period, the Maya began creating polychrome (many-colored) pottery and increasingly made it for decorative rather than practical purposes. They primarily used the colors orange, red, black, brown, grey and cream; blue was used only for pottery related to religious ceremonies and for temple frescoes and incense burners. The images on pottery were typically religious in nature, although some had geometric designs instead.

One of the most significant pieces of Maya pottery in terms of religious imagery was discovered in the Petén area of Guatemala. According to archaeologist George Stuart, it reveals "a macabre world of rite and myth. Glyphs [Maya hieroglyphic writing] suggest an Underworld setting. Among the figures around it, a jaguar writhes upon a throne of bones. Others include a skeleton in jaguar garb, and a woman with a sacrificed infant."[47]

Since the Maya had no potter's wheel, vessels were shaped laboriously with the fingers from lumps of clay. Alternatively clay was rolled into a coil that was then spiraled, pressed, and smoothed to create the sides of a vessel. However, a wide variety of shapes were created depending on region. As Dr. Peter Harrison explains:

SARCOPHAGUS DISCOVERY

Some Maya artwork has left archaeologists with more questions than answers regarding Maya society. Such an item is one of the sarcophagi found in Palenque. In his book Mysterious Maya *Dr. George Stuart describes this artifact and the mysteries it poses.*

"A broken limestone slab was found in the rubble of a collapsed building in 1974. It is unique as far as we know, for glyphs inscribed on its top follow the rectangular edge and then turn inward into a spiral. The carving has suffered from erosion but some glyphs have, tentatively, been translated: Death . . . Smoking Mirror [who was the child of] Lady MaCuc [and] the child of Lord . . . of Cobá. . . . The stone was probably a sarcophagus cover. It is small, small enough for a child. And only a child of the nobility would have been honored with such a burial. The mother shares the name Cuc, or Squirrel, with a powerful ruler of Naranjo, the Lord Zic Cuc, known as Naranjo, the Lord Zic whose marriage to a lady of Tikal, on August 28, 682, is recorded on monuments at both Cobá and Naranjo, 250 miles apart.

Who then was Smoking Mirror? The child of a ruler? Were the rulers of Cobá and Naranjo related, or allied by marriage? Did Smoking Mirror die before his time? And had he lived, would he have ruled a powerful city? Did the fortunes of a dynasty change at a princeling's death?

The glyphs are carved so that we had to walk around the stone counterclockwise several times to see them properly. It reminded me of a hetzmek ceremony; the slab of a tabletop. Did priests and Smoking Mirror's noble kin walk these same rounds many centuries ago—perhaps as part of a ceremony for his future, an aid to his journey through the Underworld?

And how soon after his death was he forgotten, or so unimportant that part of his tomb was used as a building stone?

No one knows his story."

Maya ceramics were decorated with all sorts of images and colors.

Ceramics are . . . subject to rapid change and individual expression. Each major Maya site has its own artistic expression in the rendering of details in their locally made ceramics. The overall style which emerges at a single city contains a combination of the shapes and finishes of vessels and the individual characteristics of painted decoration developed by the artisans of that city.[48]

Maya vessels could be decorated either before or after baking. Prebaking decorations included marks made with stamps or molds as well as figures appliquéd onto the vessel's sides. Post-baking decorations were engravings and/or paints. To bake the pottery, the Maya used an open bed of charcoal; they had no kilns.

In addition to bowls, plates, pots, and vases, the Maya made numerous clay figurines, some solid and some hollow. Archaeologists are unsure about their purpose. Apparently some were meant to honor the deceased, but others seem to be ceremonial. Elizabeth Benson reports:

They [the figurines] often represent human beings in ceremonial regalia.

ARCHAEOLOGICAL EVIDENCE IN CAVES

The ancient Maya apparently believed that caves provided an entrance to the Underworld, and they buried some of their dead in these places. Consequently caves have provided archaeologists with valuable information about the Maya culture. Michael Coe reports on one important cave discovery in his book The Maya.

"One . . . cave, now named Naj Tunich, was discovered in 1979 by local residents in karst [cave-riddled limestone] terrain near Poptun, in the southeastern Petén. The cave is huge, measuring 2,790 ft. (850 m) deep along its longest passage. It has ancient walls, Late Classic burials, and terminal Late Preclassic pottery, but it was apparently extensively looted before archaeologists could get to it. The importance of Naj Tunich lies in its extensive hieroglyphic texts (altogether comprising about 400 glyphs) and scenes, all executed in carbon black on the cave walls. The latter include depictions of the ball game, amorous activities . . . and Maya deities, which not unexpectedly include the Hero Twins, Hunahpu and Xbalanque. The style of the writing and painting is closely related to Late Classic vases . . . and must have been carried out by one or more artists and scribes skilled in the production of Maya books."

Some of them are ball players wearing their protective equipment, others are warriors, dancing figures, or musicians. Sometimes they represent people dressed in ordinary clothing going about everyday activities, including women, often shown grinding corn on a metate [grinding stone]. Some figures are seated on a throne or in a litter [a wooden platform used to carry someone]. There are other types of figurines that appear frequently: a woman with a child, an old man with a young woman, a hunchback, or a nude fat man. The faces and details of dress of figurines are usually quite naturalistic, often showing facial tattooing. . . . There are also various figurines representing animals. . . .

Many of these figurines [both human and animal] are sound-producing. Some are whistles with a hole to blow in or over, and others are rattles with a pellet of clay inside. The persons represented must have had some sort of significance or power . . . they may have been household gods . . . perhaps they were also symbols of a secular status [one not related to religion]. Because so many of them produce a sound, it is possible that they were used to accompany ceremonial dances or processions; they might have been connected with sympathetic magic or religious or secular ceremonies. Since a number of the whistles also have holes, so that they might be strung and hung around the neck, it has been suggested that they may have been worn by hunters who used them to imitate the call of the bird or animal they were hunting.[49]

Other figurines were clearly made to hold incense. Typically fashioned to look like the god for whom the incense was being burned, they might be used in large public rituals but more commonly appeared on small shrines for household worship. One place where such shrines were particularly popular was in the city of Mayapán, which became powerful between approximately A.D. 1200 and 1440. During that time the city had only one major temple and no ball courts, obliging its roughly twelve hundred residents to

Pictured is a Maya jade figurine. In addition to pottery, the Maya also made all types of figurines.

do most of their worship in private. Consequently archaeologists have found hundreds of Mayapán figurines during excavations of the city.

OTHER ARTWORK

There are far fewer examples of decorative Maya textiles. This does not mean that the Maya did not produce them, but rather that such items have a higher tendency to decay over time. Of the few items discovered, most were preserved in the mud at the bottom of the Well of Sacrifice. Woven cotton cloth found at this location was dyed red, yellow, and blue using various natural substances. The cloth was also embroidered to create images of people, gods, birds, fish, animals, flowers, and geometric designs. In some cases the feathers of the hummingbird, the quetzal bird, and various types of parrot—particularly the macaw—had been woven into the fabric as it was made.

Many other objects also have been found in the Well of Sacrifice. In discussing the cenote's excavation, Dr. George Stuart says, "Immense amounts of jade and some gold artifacts, articles of wood, copper, and rubber, have come from the well—along with balls of copal incense, and the bones of children thrown in alive to placate the Rain God. The material found here comes from as far away as Panama, and most of it dates from late Postclassic times."[50]

In other sites, archaeologists have found a little metalwork and woven baskets that are not especially decorative. Copper and bronze were both available during the later years of the Maya civilization, but they were mostly used to create objects like rings that were intended for personal ornamentation and rarely for weapons or tools. In contrast, the Maya created numerous flint and obsidian weapons, tools, and ornaments of a superior quality. These include spearheads and knives as well as rings and figurines depicting various animals, birds, and humans. Consequently many archaeologists have concluded that the Maya preferred to work in stone.

Of all the stones that they used, they believed jade to be the most precious. In fact, they considered it sacred. Perhaps for this reason archaeologists have recovered numerous jade items in their excavations of Maya cities, particularly in conjunction with burials. Dr. George Stuart describes the items found on a body in one sarcophagus:

> Jade disks from a diadem lay on the head, along with the collapsed fragments of a polished jade mosaic mask, and ear ornaments engraved with hieroglyphic texts. A wide band of tubular jade beads covered the chest, and other necklaces were made of beads in the shape of tiny flowers and fruit. A jade bead lay inside the mouth; ornate rings had graced all the fingers. Near the left foot lay a jade statuette of the sun god.[51]

By studying these artifacts and other items near the sarcophagus, archaeolo-

This carving of Pakal, thought to date from seventh century, was discovered at the ruins of Palenque.

gists concluded that the man who wore them was a king named Pacal, or Hand-shield, who ruled Palenque in the seventh century. His remains were found in a place they dubbed the Temple of the Inscriptions for its numerous writings. These writings combined with the temple's artwork to provide the clues necessary to deduce certain facts about Pacal's reign. Without one or the other his identity might have remained a mystery.

5 Intellectual Pursuits

Although the building materials they had on hand were relatively crude, the Maya developed the ability and the desire to create great cities. In both they were aided by their understanding of mathematics and their elegant notions of time. The former allowed them to make complex architectural calculations as well as a record of important dates and measurements. The latter encouraged them to keep such records and build monuments as testaments to their society and its beliefs. In this way the Maya's intellectual pursuits stimulated the flowering of their civilization.

MATHEMATICS

The Maya apparently adopted the mathematical system of the Olmecs, then expanded upon it to perform more advanced calculations than their predecessors. Specifically, the Olmecs used dots and bars to represent numbers, but the Maya added the concept of zero to this system. In fact, most modern scholars believe that the Maya were the first people in the world to grasp the concept of zero, which they usually depicted with the symbol of a

shell. This is quite an accomplishment considering that the ancient Greeks and Romans had not arrived at the concept of zero and therefore—despite all their other intellectual advances—could make only relatively simple arithmetic calculations.

Having a zero allowed the Maya to develop what mathematicians call a vigesimal system of counting, which uses position shifts and placeholders to represent extremely large numbers. In the Arabic system used in the Western world, the vigesimal system is based on the number 10; each movement of the number 1 to the left in a series of columns increases its power by 10. For example, 10 equals 1 x 10 or ten, 100 equals 1 x 10 x 10 or one hundred, 1,000 equals 1 x 10 x 10 x 10 or one thousand, and so on. For the Maya, each movement of their symbol for 1, a dot, to one column higher on a vertical stack of columns increases that dot's power by 20. Therefore a dot in the lowest position equals one, in the next lowest 1 x 20 or twenty, in the next column up 1 x 20 x 20 or four hundred, in the next 1 x 20 x 20 x 20 or eight thousand, and so on.

Moreover, dots were placed horizontally, and five dots equaled one horizontal bar. Therefore the number 9 was written as one horizontal bar with four dots lined up side by side above it. The number 19 was written as three horizontal bars stacked one atop the other, again with four dots lined up above the top bar (5 + 5 + 5 + 4). Although the Maya symbol for zero was most commonly a drawing that modern scholars have called a shell, some regions used other symbols.

Using this system, then, the number 819 would be written from the bottom to the top of a numerical column as three bars with four dots over them (19), then a shell as a placeholder (0), then two dots (400 + 400) above all. The number 16,422 would be written from bottom to top as two dots (2), one dot (20), one dot (400), and finally two dots (8,000 + 8,000) atop the column.

As with the Arabic system, the Maya system employed "borrowing" or "carrying" numbers from one place to another to perform calculations. However, whatever was borrowed or carried was expressed as a multiple of 20 instead of 10. In addition, Maya in different regions created variations on this system, perhaps reversing the order of the columns or using glyphs instead of bars and dots.

A glyph is a carved figure in relief, and since the Maya used calendar dates on their stelae and other carvings, these pictures were another way to make the stones decorative. Generally, glyph images are of gods, usually just the heads but sometimes the bodies as well. For example, instead of a dot, the number 1 might be represented by a glyph of the moon goddess. However, because the Maya usually insisted on creating symmetry within their work, sometimes they added meaningless glyphs to numbers on a stelae in order to make it look aesthetically pleasing. This has caused archaeologists studying the Maya mathematical system some confusion.

CALENDAR UNITS

The Maya probably used their counting system to calculate numbers related to their trading practices, employing cacao beans or grains of maize as visual aids. However, the surviving evidence of this system comes from stelae, codices, and other ancient artifacts. In these, most of the concerns related to mathematics involve time rather than economics.

The Maya employed their base-20 mathematical system to create a complex calendar, although they varied it somewhat in accordance with their understanding of astronomy. The Maya knew, for example, that the solar year was approximately 365 days. Therefore while a day, or kin, was worth 1, and the next unit, uinal—the equivalent of a month—was worth 20, the next unit, the tun, was not 20 x 20, or 400, as with counting, but rather 360, the closest number to 365 that was still divisible by 20. For longer periods of time, they reverted to their standard base-20 system, so that their units were as follows:

20 kins	= 1 uinal	= 20 days
18 uinals	= 1 tun	= 360 days
20 tuns	= 1 katun	= 7,200 days
20 katuns	= 1 baktun	= 144,000 days

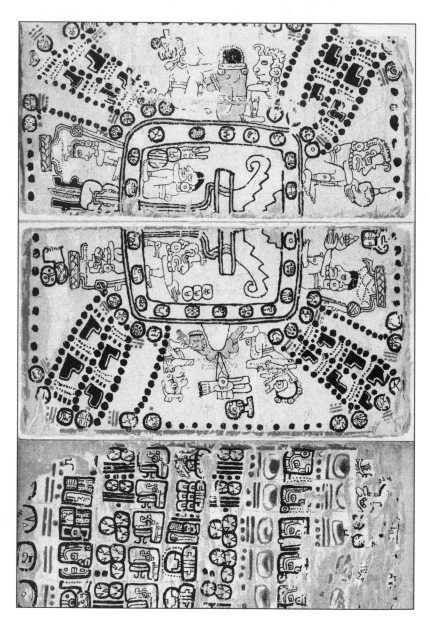

Pictured is a sample from the intricately designed Codex Cortesianus, *which provided insight into the Maya number and calendar system.*

20 baktuns	= 1 pictun	=	2,880,000 days
20 pictuns	= 1 calabtun	=	57,600,000 days
20 calabtuns	= 1 kinchiltun	=	1,152,000,000 days
20 kinchiltuns	= 1 alautun	=	23,040,000,000 days

However, the Maya calendar was even more complex than even this counting system implies. Whereas Westerners keep track only of the cycle of the sun—the solar year—the Maya kept track of more than one cycle based on the movements of not only the sun but also the moon, the planet Venus, and other celestial objects. These cycles in turn were used to calculate greater cycles. Consequently Sylvanus G. Morley and George W. Brainerd say:

> The Maya calendar was far more complex than the system we use, for it served a variety of purposes, both practical and esoteric (such as astrological divination). The full knowledge of the Maya calendar must have been guarded by the ruling elite, since it was undoubtedly a source of great power. The calendar demonstrated to the populace that the rulers held close communion with the supernatural forces that governed the cosmos. One might assume, however, that even the poorest farmer had some knowledge of the basic system, by which to guide his family's daily life.[52]

The three most commonly used cycles were the Sacred Almanac of 260 days, the Vague Year, or *haab*, of 365 days, and the 52-year Calendar Round. In addition, the Maya developed a chronological system, called the Long Count (or Initial Series) by modern scholars, and several derivatives of

---

NEW KNOWLEDGE OF GLYPHS

In recent years experts in Maya glyphs have discovered that certain markings indicate that an item belonged to a particular person. In his book Daily Life in Maya Civilization, *Professor Robert Sharer explains how this has helped to identify certain tombs.*

"Numerous objects have painted or carved glyphs, many of which are now being read as 'name tags' that accompany the owner's name. For example, the glyphs on a jade ear spool excavated at Altun Ha, Belize, read *u tup,* or 'his ear spool.' Glyphs on incised bone offerings in Ah Cacau's tomb at Tikal include the phrase *u bak,* or 'his bone.' Pottery vessels are often tagged with *u lak,* or 'his bowl.' The function of the tagged object may also be given, and in the glyphs on an Early Classic bowl from Rio Azul labeled as a pot for *kakaw* ('chocolate'). The tomb long proposed to be that of Tikal ruler Yax Kin is verified by a text on a painted vase from the tomb stating that it is the 'chocolate pot of Yax Kin Kan Chac, 3 katun divine ruler of Tikal.' The scene on the vessel shows Yax Kin seated on a cushion accompanied by a small pot decorated with the Naranjo emblem glyph, identifying it as a tribute from Naranjo to the Tikal ruler."

the Long Count in order to calculate and record the exact number of days elapsed from a particular point in time.

THE SACRED ALMANAC

The Sacred Almanac, also called the Sacred Year or tzolkin, had twenty day-names (each apparently also the name of a god) and thirteen day-numbers as labels for its 260 days. These names and numbers ran concurrently and were therefore combined in sequence. For example, the first day-name was Imix, and the first time Imix appeared in a 260-day year it was labeled 1 Imix. The next day-name was Ik and the next day-number 2, so the second day of the year was labeled 2 Ik. The third day-name was Akbal and the next day-number 3, so the third day of the year was labeled 3 Akbal. When the numbers 1 through 13 had been used once, the count of day-numbers was started again at 1, and Ix, the fourteenth name on the list of day-names, was paired with 1, or 1 Ix. By the time the day-number had progressed from this point to 8, the twenty day-names had been used once, and the next date was 8 Imix. Only after all 260 days of the year had passed did 1 Imix appear again, whereupon the cycle repeated.

The full list of day-names is as follows:
Imix
Ik
Akbal
Kan
Chicchan
Cimi
Manik
Lamat
Muluc
Oc
Chuen
Eb
Ben
Ix
Men
Cib
Caban
Etz-nab
Cauac
Ahau

THE VAGUE YEAR

The Sacred Almanac was so named because it was used to record dates related to the sacred lives of the Maya, including yearly rituals and birthdates. In making such records no other notations were needed except the Sacred Year. However, for any matters related to civic events, kings' reigns, and Maya history, the Vague Year, or *haab*, had to be employed. Based on the solar year, the Vague Year had 19 months; the first 18 had 20 days each and the final one had 5 days, for a total of 365 days in the year. This short last month, called Uayeb, was considered unlucky, a time when people avoided doing things for fear they would turn out badly.

The nineteen months of the Vague Year were named as follows:
Pop
Uo
Zip

Zotz
Tzec
Xul
Yaxkin
Mol
Chen
Yax
Zac
Ceh
Mac
Kankin
Muan
Pax
Kayab
Cumku
Uayeb

The days of this year were designated by the month-name combined with a number from 0 to 19 for the 20-day months and from 0 to 4 for the 5-day month. The first day of the Vague Year, for example, was 0 Pop, the second 1 Pop, and so on. The first day of the following month was 0 Uo, the second 1 Uo, and so on. The Maya began with 0 because, as Dr. Thomas Gann explains,

> they counted only elapsed time, and the first day would not be called 1 Pop until it was completed. We, too, to a certain extent count only elapsed time, for we speak of 11:30 A.M., whereas we mean we are half way through the twelfth hour. Similarly we do not speak of its being 12 o'clock until the twelfth hour is completed. However, we are not consistent as we speak of the day being the 21st of the month before that day is completed.[53]

In writing the date of a particular day on stelae, the Maya combined the notations of the Sacred Year and the Vague Year. In other words, a date had a day-name, day-number, month-name, and month-number. This full date was determined by keeping track of the progression of two cycles of days, the Sacred Year and the Vague Year, which ran concurrently as though each were on a wheel whose cogs meshed with the other. However, the two wheels did not have the same number of cogs; the Vague Year had 105 more days than the Sacred Year. This means that at the end of one Sacred Year the Vague Year would already have advanced 105 cogs into a new year. Because of this, the same date—the same combination of day-name, day-number, month-name, and month-number—would only come around once every fifty-two years.

Modern scholars call this fifty-two-year period the Calendar Round. For them it is just a helpful way to date Maya carvings. For the ancient Maya, however, the Calendar Round probably had religious significance. Scholars like Sylvanus Morley and George Brainerd support this theory because they know that a similar calendar had religious significance for other people in Mesoamerica. They explain:

> The Mexica (Aztecs), for example, conceived time as an endless succession of these 52-year periods. . . . The Mexica had two special glyphs for this period, arising from their beliefs concerning it. The first was a knot indicating that the bundle of 52 years had been tied up, and the second

227	228

229	230	231	232
233	234	235	236
237	238	239	240
241	242	243	244

These glyphs represent eighteen of the nineteen months of the Maya Vague Year, or haab.

was the fire drill and stick for kindling the Sacred Fire. The Mexica believed that the world would come to an end at the close of one of these 52-year periods, and on the last night of the *xiuhmolpilli* ["year bundle"], the population of Tenochtitlan (Mexico City) withdrew to the hills surrounding the city to await the dawn. When the sun rose on that morning, there was general rejoicing, the Sacred Fire was rekindled, the houses were cleaned and set in order, and the business of life resumed. The gods had given mankind another 52-year lease on life.[54]

THE LONG COUNT

In the Maya calendar each Calendar Round day also had an equivalent Long Count date, which fixed it in a particular point in time relative to a major event in

Maya history. Modern scholars believe that this event might have been the creation of the world according to Maya cosmology. The Maya calendar centered on this event much the way the Gregorian calendar proceeds from the birth of Jesus, arbitrarily beginning its count in the year that sixteenth-century scholars believed Jesus had been born. Morley and Brainerd report that many other cultures also relate their calendar to such a significant event:

> The Greeks reckoned time by four-year periods called Olympiads, beginning with the earliest Olympic festival for which the winner's name was known, in 776 B.C. Other chronologies begin with hypothetical starting points, for example, the supposed date of the creation of the world. The era of Constantinople, the chronological system used by the Greek Church, begins with a creation date corresponding to 5509 B.C. The Jewish cal-endar begins with an equivalent date of 3761 B.C.[55]

The fixed point of the Maya Long Count corresponds to a day in 3114 B.C. It is a moment when one of their cycles of thirteen baktuns, which is roughly 5,128 solar years or 1,872,000 days, ends and the next begins. This date was labeled 13.0.0.0.0 4 Ahau 8 Cumku.

The Maya put their Long Count date—a notation similar to the Gregorian calendar's B.C. or A.D.—in front of their Calendar Round date. Morley and Brainerd explain its appearance:

> Great-cycle dates open most Classic Maya inscriptions. . . . Long-count texts first appear on Late Preclassic monuments in the southern Maya area, and are later found throughout the Maya lowlands during the Classic period, providing dedicatory dates for monuments and other inscriptions. The long-count date fixes a

MAYA GLYPHS

After visiting the Maya of the Yucatán in 1586 Spanish priest Alonso Ponce praised their writing abilities in his Relación, *as quoted by Sylvanus G. Morley in the introduction to his English version of the* Popol Vuh.

"They had characters and letters, with which they wrote their histories and ceremonies, and the order of the sacrifices to their idols and their calendar in books made of the bark of a certain tree. . . . Only the priests of the idols (who in that language are called 'ahkines') and some principal Indians understood these letters and characters."

given calendar-round day within the great cycle of thirteen baktuns (1,872,000 days). It is preceded by a standardized and oversized glyph, usually four times as large as the following hieroglyphs, known as the introductory glyph. . . . The following five glyph blocks record the number of baktuns, katuns, tuns, uinals, and kins that have elapsed from the beginning of the current great cycle. . . . The first part of the calendar-round date, the almanac designation, follows, and after a series of intervening glyphs the second part of the calendar round date, the *haab* designation, closes the long count.[56]

Because the glyphs of the Long Count appear as a series at the front of the date, some modern scholars call the Long Count the Initial Series. There is a Secondary Series as well, a kind of short cut to get from one date to another. Morley and Brainerd explain why this was necessary: "To express a single day by means of the long count, ten different glyphs were necessary. This method of dating was accurate but cumbersome, and its repetition for every additional date in an inscription was superfluous. If one date in an inscription was fixed, other dates could be calculated from it."[57]

The Secondary Series allows this calculation by providing a number of days, also called distance numbers, to be counted either backward or forward to reach the fixed, or base, date. Scholars have disagreed about why the Maya developed this concept of deriving dates. Some suggest that by referring readers of stelae inscriptions to long-distant dates the Maya may have been attempting to show an ancestral connection between the rulers featured in the stelae and their gods. Morley and Brainerd expand on this idea:

> Initially, secondary-series dates were thought to be a calendar-correction formula, somewhat like our leap-year correction. However, the known instances of secondary-series dates span intervals as short as one day and perhaps as long as millions of years. Thus the secondary series probably served a variety of purposes, but in most cases they seem to refer to cyclical antecedents [predecessors] used by the lords to legitimize their royal ancestry and their right to rule. In some cases these inscriptions refer to dates deep in the mythical past.[58]

THE SHORT COUNT

Toward the end of the Late Classic Period of Maya history the Maya developed a shorter system of noting the Long Count date, reducing the number of glyphs required to indicate it. Called the Short Count, it was this method that the Spanish encountered when they conquered the Maya. Although Bishop Landa had nothing but scorn for the Maya religion, he was greatly impressed by the culture's inventiveness in terms of timekeeping. He wrote:

> Not only did the Indians have a count for the year and months . . . but they

also had a certain method of counting time and their affairs by their ages, which they counted by twenty-year periods, counting thirteen twenties, with one of the twenty signs of their months, which they call Ahau, not in order, but going backward. . . . In their language they call these [periods] katuns, with these they make a calculation of their ages that is marvelous, thus it was easy for . . . [an] old man . . . to recall events that had taken place three hundred years be-fore. Had I not known of these calculations, I should not have believed it possible to recall thus after such a period.[59]

ASTRONOMY

The Maya had other notations besides the Long Count and the Short Count. One of these is the Lunar Series, a series of up to eight glyphs dealing with the cycles of the moon in relation to a particular date.

This Maya observatory at Chichén-Itzá was used to collect astronomical data on numerous celestial bodies.

There is ample evidence, both on stelae and in the few surviving Maya codices, that the Maya applied their mathematical skills to calculations related to various celestial bodies. Anthropologist Michael Coe describes an example of the Maya's knowledge of astronomy:

Of great interest to Mayanists and astronomers alike have been the eclipse tables recorded on seven pages of the Dresden Codex. These cover a cycle of 405 lunations [lunar months] or 11,960 days, which conveniently enough equals 46 x 260 days—a kind of formula with which the Maya were deeply concerned, for such equations enabled them to coordinate the movements of the heavenly bodies with their most sacred ritual period. The ancients had found out, at least by the mid-eighth century A.D. but possibly much earlier, that lunar and solar eclipses could only occur within plus or minus 18 days of the node (when the moon's path crosses the apparent path of the sun); and this is what the tables are, a statement of when such events were likely.[60]

Another section of the Dresden Code deals with solar eclipses, still another with the movements of Venus. The Maya made additional calculations related to the movements of Mars and to a lesser extent Mercury, and there is some evidence that they considered the movements of Jupiter as well. They used their knowledge of astronomy for divination, making predictions regarding the reigns of kings and determining the best days to hold important events. They also constructed buildings in accordance with their desire to study celestial bodies and the resulting astronomical observations. Coe reports:

The [modern] astronomer Anthony Aveni and the architect Horst Hartung have determined that the ancient Maya used buildings and doorways and windows within them for astronomical sightings, especially of Venus. At Uxmal, for instance, all buildings are aligned in the same direction, except the House of the Governor. A perpendicular taken [projected] from the central doorway of this structure reaches a solitary mound about 3½ miles away; Venus would have risen precisely above the mound when the planet reached its southerly extreme in A.D. 750. In collaboration with Sharon Gibbs, they have shown that in the case of the Caracol at Chichén Itzá, the whole building is aligned to the northerly extremes of Venus at about A.D. 1000, as is a diagonal sightline in one of the windows of the tower top; another diagonal sightline matched the planet's setting position when it attained its maximum southerly declination.[61]

Some modern scholars also believe that the Maya had a form of astrology that included a zodiac—an imaginary belt in the heavens divided into segments named after certain constellations, which in turn were named after beings they resembled. Coe says:

Did the Maya have . . . [a zodiac]? On this subject there is little agreement, but some have seen an indication of a partial zodiac on a damaged page of the Paris Codex, which shows a scorpion, turtle, and rattlesnake pendant from a celestial band. Very little is known of star lore among the Maya, but they did have constellations called *tzab* ("rattlesnake rattle," the Pleiades) and *ac* ("turtle," made up of stars in Gemini), with which they could tell the time of night; so a "zodiac" is quite probable.[62]

Many modern scholars find the Maya's knowledge of astronomy impressive particularly because the Maya had no telescopes or even lenses for observing the heavens. Apparently they set up pairs of crossed sticks in temple windows as fixed points, then observed the movements of celestial objects in relation to these fixed points. Of the success of this work Elizabeth Benson says:

> The Maya were extraordinary astronomers, and the date inscriptions on the stelae were often followed by astronomical data. It is no easy feat to make observations of sunrises and sunsets, eclipses, the movements of Venus, etc., in a country where it rains for nearly nine months of the year. It is also remarkable that the Maya were able to make astronomical observations with such minimal equipment. . . . [Moreover,] one must remember that the Maya had no concept of a round earth. The movements of heavenly bodies were not thought of as revolutions but as events that repeated themselves in a given pattern, as time itself was a repeating pattern.[63]

WRITING

It has taken scholars many years to piece together what they now know about Maya astronomy and mathematics because of the difficulty they had deciphering the glyphs of the codices and other Maya writings. In fact, even now about 15 percent of Maya inscriptions are not fully understood. The first glyphs to be deciphered were those related to numbers, directions, colors, the calendar, and astronomy, in that order. Glyphs representing other concepts have been more difficult to interpret.

Deciphering Maya glyphs is very difficult because some glyphs are pictographic, which means that their images represent entire words or names, while others are syllabic, which means that they represent syllables and/or linguistic sounds (phonetics). To complicate matters further the same concepts may be represented in more than one way. As an example, Coe says, "the name of the great Palenque ruler Pacal ('Hand-shield') could be written either as a picture of a hand-shield, or phonetically as *par-ca-l(a)*, or both."[64] Moreover, the meaning of some glyphs can change in the presence of others. Therefore a good translation of the meaning of a glyph in one inscription does not necessarily help scholars

THE BOOKS OF CHILAM BALAM

One important source of information on Maya life is a collection of works known as the Books of Chilam Balam. Some scholars say that Chilam Balam was a famous Maya prophet, others that he was the priest of Chilam Balam, a ruling lord of the Yucatec of the Yucatán peninsula, and performed divination ceremonies to foresee the future. In either case, most scholars, including Michael Coe, believe that although these works date from the seventeenth and eighteenth centuries they are copies or derivations of manuscripts written hundreds of years earlier. If this is so, then some parts of the Books of Chilam Balam appear to have predicted the Spanish Conquest. For example, the following poem, as quoted in Coe's book The Maya, *seems to foretell the Maya's flight into the forests to engage in guerrilla warfare with Spanish soldiers.*

Eat, eat, thou has bread;
Drink, drink, thou has water;
On that day, dust possesses the earth;
On that day, a blight is on the face of the earth,
On that day, a cloud rises,
On that day, a mountain rises,
On that day, a strong man seizes the land,
On that day, things fall to ruin,
On that day, the tender leaf is destroyed,
On that day, the dying eyes are closed,
On that day, three signs are on the tree,
On that day, three generations hang there,
On that day, the battle flag is raised,
And they are scattered afar in the forests.

determine the meaning of the same character in another passage.

The deciphering of glyphs has its own problems. Not only did the Spaniards destroy many Maya writings, but their impact on Maya culture influenced the translation of surviving Maya glyphs. For example, the Spanish soldiers and priests introduced new elements into the Maya language that might have broken its connection to the ancient tongue. Consequently, as Elizabeth Benson reports:

"The modern Maya language gives clues and is helpful in suggesting both meanings and pronunciation, but no real bridge has yet been found between modern and ancient Maya, and the scholar must always be wary of natural growth and change in the language and of new words introduced from outside."[65]

If one effect of the Spaniards' occupation was intentional, apparently another was not. Bishop Diego de Landa misled researchers of Maya writings by widely disseminating a Maya "alphabet" that subsequently proved to be seriously flawed. He claimed that he was given this key to translating Maya glyphs by the son of a Maya chief, but some scholars now think that he lied for reasons unknown.

As Michael Coe reports, "Several extremely distinguished Maya scholars have stumbled badly in trying to read the codices and the inscriptions with Landa's treacherous 'ABC,' while some have gone so far as to declare it a complete fraud."[66]

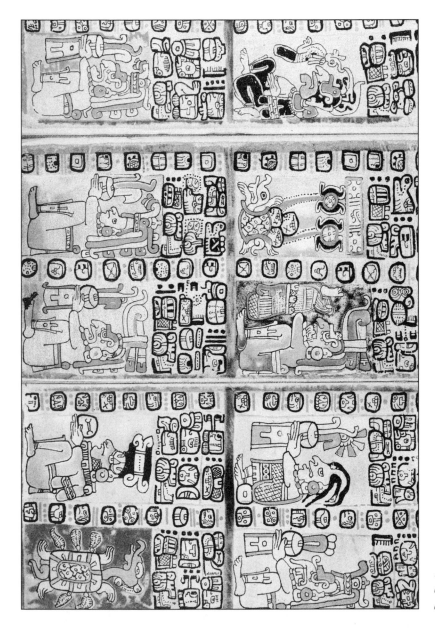

Deciphering Maya glyphs is difficult because some glyphs are pictographic.

Thus for a variety of reasons the Western world will never know the full extent of the Maya's knowledge. However, in recent years great strides have been made in deciphering their glyphs. Scholars have identified some of the glyphs related to battles, bloodletting, royal duties and dynastic titles, family relationships, and personal names. Therefore some people believe that all Maya glyphs will eventually be deciphered, leading to a more complete picture of their ancient civilization.

6 The Decline of the Maya Civilization

Between roughly A.D. 800 and 900—the Late Classic period of Maya history—the Maya civilization underwent a decline that brought with it the end of many of its great cities. In fact, during this period the heart of Maya territory, the Central area where the most powerful and glorious cities then existed, was completely abandoned. Professor Robert Sharer has called this event "one of the most profound cultural failures in human history."[67]

After this failure, during the subsequent Early Post-Classic period (approximately A.D. 900 to 1200) and Late Post-Classic period (approximately A.D. 1200 to 1500), the cities of the Maya who lived in the northern Yucatán peninsula and the Guatemala highlands were taken over by outsiders. Michael Coe sums up their plight: "By the close of the tenth century the destiny of the once proud and independent Maya had fallen into the hands of grim militarists from the highlands of central Mexico, where a new order of men had replaced the intellectual rulers of Classic times."[68]

Coe reports that the city of Chichén-Itzá was taken over by the Toltec, a violent people from Mexico whose rule was marked by internal conflicts, and the city

of Mayapán was taken over by the Itzá, another violent Mesoamerican culture about which little is known. During their occupations of these and other Maya cities these invaders created hybrid Maya-Mexican cultures, so that in effect the Maya culture ceased to exist.

Both of these invaders lost their hold over the Maya by the beginning of the thirteenth century, and Maya culture reasserted itself. It was not, however, the same culture as before. Coe reports:

> In place of a single, united kingdom were now sixteen rival statelets, each jealous of the power and lands of the other, and only too eager to go to war in asserting its claims. Yet it is also true that the culture of the times, for whatever it was worth, was Maya, for much of what the Mexicans had brought was already forgotten and traditional Maya ways of doing things were substituted for imported habits.[69]

Nonetheless, the Maya no longer had what could be called a true civilization. It was disjoined and disunited, and in this condition it was no match for the Spanish invaders of the sixteenth century. The

This painting depicts Toltec warriors attacking a Maya village.

Maya did put up a good fight against these invaders, however. Shortly after discovering the Yucatán in 1517, Spanish explorer Hernández de Córdoba died of wounds he received from Maya warriors. According to Coe other Spanish met similar fates:

> [Destroying the Maya] was no easy task [for the Spanish], for unlike the mighty Aztec, there was no overall authority which could be toppled, bringing an empire with it. Nor did

the Maya fight in the accepted fashion. Attacking the Spaniards at night, plotting ambushes and traps, they were jungle guerrillas in a familiar modern tradition. Accordingly, it was not until 1542 that the hated foreigners managed to establish a capital, Merida; even so revolt continued to plague the Spaniards throughout the sixteenth century. . . . [Moreover,] the Maya are, for all their apparent docility, the toughest Indians of Mesoamerica, and the struggle against European civilization never once halted [after the conquest].[70]

Coe goes on to explain that the Maya continued to fight Europeans during the nineteenth century, when they came very close to retaking the Yucatán peninsula, and to fight Mexican rule during the early twentieth century. In fact, he says that "only in the last few decades have . . . remote Maya villagers begun to accept the rule of Mexico."[71] But if the Maya are indeed such tough people—as is perhaps evidenced by the fact that they continue to survive in Central America today, despite their years of adversity—then why did their great civilization decline during the ninth century?

STELAE DATES

Although they have developed many theories about this decline, modern scholars do not really know why the Maya civilization failed, just as they don't know what destroyed the culture of the Maya's predecessors, the Olmec. In fact, many experts in Mesoamerican culture, including Elizabeth Benson, have called the Maya's decline "one of the great mysteries of archaeology."[72] However, archaeological evidence does provide some clues regarding what might have happened to the Maya between the years A.D. 800 and 900.

This evidence comes primarily from the amount of and dates on stelae produced during this period. During the year 790, at least 19 cities erected new stelae,

THE CRUELTIES OF SPANISH SOLDIERS

It took twenty-four years for the Spanish to conquer the Maya, and even then some of them eluded capture. When Spanish soldiers did find some resistant Maya they typically treated them with great cruelty. In a letter to the Spanish government, a Franciscan missionary complained about the atrocities he witnessed. This passage quoted in George Stuart's Mysterious Maya *accuses a Spanish officer of terrible acts in the city of Chetumal.*

"Tying them [the Maya] to stakes, he cut the breasts off many women, and hands, noses, and ears off the men . . . and he threw [women] in the lakes to drown merely to amuse himself. . . . [The Maya who learned of these events] fled from all this and did not sow their crops, and all died of hunger."

but in 869 only three apparently did. The city of Piedras Negras erected its last stelae in 795, the city of Palenque in 799, the cities of Bonampak and Copán in 800, Quiriguá in 805, Tikal in 869, and Uaxactun in 889. The last known Initial Series date on any stela was A.D. 909, so it appears that none was erected after that date. Archaeological evidence also suggests that no new buildings or additions or modifications to existing buildings were made after that date.

By studying the order in which Maya cities stopped growing archaeologists have discerned a pattern to their demise: The decline began in lowland areas and then moved into the highlands. In other words, the first cities affected were on the perimeter of Maya lands, the last at their heart.

POSSIBLE ATTACKERS

Some scholars have therefore concluded that the reason Maya cities abandoned construction during the ninth century was foreign invasion. Perhaps some neighbor of the Maya attacked them at a shared border, then took over city after city on their march to the center of the Maya civilization. The Maya cities that survived would have been distant from this conflict but still affected by the war, given the interconnectedness between Maya states due to trade.

There is no evidence of who the Maya's ninth century attackers might have been, if indeed there were any. However, scholars believe that the most likely attackers would have been the people of the city of Teotihuacán in the Valley of Mexico. It appears that the Maya had a close relationship with these people, because Maya pottery and stelae from the fifth century display qualities similar to the artwork of Teotihuacán. Consequently Elizabeth Benson, an expert on pre-Columbian cultures, theorizes that the Maya and the people of Teotihuacán might have fought with one another, particularly since the Teotihuacán culture disappeared around the time the Maya culture began to decline. Could the Maya have annihilated the Teotihuacán during a war? Benson says:

> Throughout Maya history there was at least occasional contact with Teotihuacán and the Valley of Mexico . . . [and] four stelae have motifs identified with Teotihuacán. . . . What sort of influence do these borrowings reflect? Was it simply fashionable to imitate the art of Teotihuacán at this period? Were there actually artists from Teotihuacán [in Tikal, where the stelae were found], or were Tikal artists trained at Teotihuacán? Was this influence transmitted through Kaminaljuyú, in the Highland area, which also shows an influence from Teotihuacán in its art? Did this artistic influence reflect a deeper tie with Teotihuacán? . . . Kaminaljuyú was influenced by Teotihuacán at various times throughout its history and was open to contact with central Mexico, contact that may ultimately have been disruptive to the entire area.[73]

An archaeologist takes readings of the electromagnetic fields of the soil in an attempt to determine what caused the fall of the Maya civilization.

However, Benson adds that some unknown Mesoamerican people could have attacked the Maya. She and other scholars note that stelae in two Maya cities, Seibal and the Altar de Sacrificios on the southern edge of the Central area, show figures that are definitely non-Maya. Dr. George Stuart describes the stelae at Seibal, which date from A.D. 751 to 869:

"Foreigners" on the Seibal stelae wear Classic Maya regalia, but they have non-Maya faces; some have mustaches. They seem to have come from the Puuc area and taken over Seibal by 830. Some traits on the Seibal carvings imply invaders from the Gulf Coast of distant Veracruz as well.[74]

Because the artwork at Seibal shows a blend of Maya and Mexican influences, some scholars suggest that the foreigners in Seibal were not there as conquerors but as people seeking shelter from attack themselves. The city is spread out over several steep hills which would have been

WARFARE WITH OTHER CITIES

During the Post-Classic period, the Maya often warred with their neighbors. Bishop de Landa wrote about one conflict that occurred while the Spanish were trying to take over Maya lands, as quoted by Elizabeth Benson in her book The Maya World.

"There was a drought, and as the inhabitants had wasted their maize in the wars with the Spaniards, such a famine befell them that they were forced to eat the bark of trees, especially of one which they call kumche, the inside of which is soft and tender. And on account of this famine, the Xiu, who are the lords of [the city of] Mani, resolved to offer solemn sacrifice to their idols, and brought slaves of both sexes to throw into the well of Chichén Itzá. And they were obliged to pass by the town of the Cocom lords, who were their declared enemies, and thinking that at such a time they would not renew their old quarrels, they sent to ask permission to go through their lands; and the Cocom deceived them by a kind answer, and giving them lodging all together in a large house, they set it on fire and killed those who escaped."

easy to defend from invaders, so perhaps the Maya allowed some non-Maya friends to join them as residents of Seibal during a war. In any case, archaeological evidence suggests that newcomers quickly took over the Seibal government. According to Dr. George Stuart, "The invaders became the elite of Seibal. Over a few decades they erected its most imposing and elegant buildings. This prosperity would endure till the last stela was set up sometime near A.D. 900."[75]

DROUGHT, DISEASE, AND DEATH

Another theory regarding why the Maya civilization might have declined has to do

with drought. There is some evidence that Mesoamerica experienced a prolonged drought beginning around A.D. 850; Maya skeletons of this time show signs of severe malnutrition, and population seems to have declined. According to some estimates the Maya population decreased from 3 million to 450,000. Therefore, it is possible that the cities died out because there was not enough population to sustain them.

However, some scholars argue that this decline in population was not due to food scarcity but to disease. Elizabeth Benson disagrees with this theory, "There is no evidence of pre-Conquest mass burials that would indicate a serious epidemic, nor has any clue to serious disease been found in skeletal material."[76] Similarly, Benson discounts the theory that some environmental catastrophe, such as an earthquake, flood, or climate change, might have damaged Maya food sources, because there is no ecological evidence of such an event. She also dismisses theories suggesting that the Maya's agricultural practices depleted the fertility of their soil, saying that these practices "could have supported the population with no deleterious effect on the land, and at least the contrary has not been proven."[77]

However, scholar John W.G. Lowe does support the theory that agricultural practices led to the Maya's decline. According to Coe, Lowe believes that the collapse of the Maya civilization progressed as follows:

> Between A.D. 672 and 751 . . . the number of communities carving new monuments continued to increase, but new construction took place only in already-established cities: Maya civilization had ceased to expand geographically. From 751 to about 790, long-standing trade alliances began to break down, interstate trade declined, and conflicts between neighboring city-states increased. . . . From 790 to 830, the death rate of cities outstripped the birth rate, while after 830 construction stopped throughout the Central Area, with the exception of peripherally located sites. . . . Lowe [says that this abrupt end] . . . was brought about by the mutually enforcing interaction of several factors, set in motion by population growth,

particularly among the élite, and by food shortages. . . . [These shortages would have been caused by] declining per capita [agricultural] production through stress on the soil and through a labor shortage caused by the diversion of field hands to the élite centers to satisfy the cultural demands of the burgeoning upper class.[78]

PEASANT REVOLT

Whereas Lowe believes that the Maya not only depleted their soil but experienced a shortage of workers because of an increased demand by the elite for household servants, other scholars have suggested that perhaps those servants were to blame for the Maya's decline in another way—by revolting against the elite. However, there is no evidence that a peasant revolution took place among the Maya, particularly since, as archaeologist Richard E.W. Adams points out, their decline was "a demographic, cultural, and social catastrophe in which elite and peasant went down together."[79] Additionally, as Elizabeth Benson notes, the post-decline Maya culture shows no evidence of being shaped by the nonelite as would be expected after a revolt, or even that the Maya culture survived at all in the affected areas. She says:

> If the Maya decline were simply a matter of revolt, it would seem that, even allowing for the clean broom of revolution, the traditions, although

possibly transformed, would have been perpetuated in some way. For example, one would expect the small centers to have continued functioning even after the major centers were abandoned. It is the abruptness of the cessation of all civic activity that is strange.[80]

TRADING PRACTICES

Instead the Maya in certain cities and their surrounding villages simply disappeared. Again, no one knows why; however, there does seem to be some connection between what happened and the Maya's economy. While at the University of Arizona in the 1970s anthropologist William Rathje studied the pattern of Maya city failure and realized that the first cities abandoned were those whose main trading items were luxuries—usually decorative pottery and goods related to religion—rather than essentials like food, salt, or obsidian (for weapons and tools). Therefore he believes that some economic disaster occurred among the Maya around the time of their downfall, so luxury items were no longer in demand. He explains:

[Cities like] Tikal were able to produce what I call a Barbie Doll cult complex based on their own local cult items. When consumers purchase a Barbie Doll, they do not buy one doll. They purchase into a whole system of optional but related sets of clothes and furniture for Barbie, friends and relatives for her, and clothes and furniture for Barbie's friends and relatives. . . . [Barbie's outfits are like] pottery and other portable cult paraphernalia, an exotic writing system, stelae. . . . In the climate [social conditions] that preceded the collapse, this sort of thing

Some scholars feel that the collapse of the Maya economy led to the decline of the Mayan civilization.

simply wasn't enough to guarantee survival.[81]

In other words, people stopped building stelae because they couldn't afford them, and they stopped buying and therefore producing pottery for the same reason. Without the income generated by trade the large cities—which were essentially marketplaces as well as religious centers—became worthless.

Because of studies like Rathje's many other scholars have developed theories connecting the Maya's decline to the economy. Some, like Rathje, suggest that the items produced by the Maya fell out of favor, thereby causing their civilization's collapse. Others have theorized that the Mesoamerican trading network changed its routes, perhaps incorporating more sea travel, and that the Maya, no longer at its center, were compromised economically.

Still others have suggested that the Mayan economy weakened, which caused the trading network to collapse because, as with most large trading networks, when one member becomes distressed the entire system is hurt. This might explain why other cultures such as the one in the city of Teotihuacán also disappeared around this period, but cities in the northern Yucatán peninsula and Guatemala highlands, away from conventional trading routes, did not fail along with their Central Area counterparts. Being less dependent on trade for their success, the more distant cities might have been spared the economic consequences of a breakdown of Central Area networks.

MANY REASONS

The most common view among scholars today, however, is that the Maya experienced a combination of problems that ultimately brought the demise of their culture. Elizabeth Benson explains the logic behind this view:

> The reasons for the decline of the Maya civilization must relate to the entire Central area over a period of a century, because a local explanation for one site or another at a single moment in time is not satisfactory. The collapse of the Central area culture is all of a piece, and yet the last dated stelae appear over a hundred-year period; like lights going out one by one, these centers died within this time span. It is tempting to search for a single romantic mystery, but to do so does not seem realistic. The factors causing the rise of the Classic Maya civilization in the Lowlands were complex and mysterious, and this must be equally true of the decline.[82]

Similarly, Linda Schele and David Freidel, who have studied the Maya city of Copán extensively, say that that city was subjected to a variety of factors that led to its demise. They report that studies of the Maya's remains, artifacts, and environment show that the Maya experienced malnutrition, sickness, battles, and a dwindling food supply due to erosion and other agricultural problems. Skeletons of the elite also indicate that they were in better physical condition than the nonelite and most likely took advantage of their position. All of these environmental and social problems, Schele and Freidel suggest, would have been blamed on Maya kings:

> The collapse [of Maya civilization] . . . came from a crisis of faith. The king held his power as the . . . avatar of the gods. . . . Ecological and political disaster could be placed directly at his feet as proof of his failure to sustain his privileged communication with the gods. . . . [Meanwhile the elite members of society] were growing rapidly in both numbers and privilege. Averaging ten centimeters taller than the rest of the population, they enjoyed the best food, the greatest portion of the wealth, and the best chance of having children who survived to adulthood. Since everyone born to a noble family could exercise elite prerogatives, it did not take too many centuries of prosperity for there to be an aristocracy of sufficient size to make itself a nuisance to governments and a burden to farmers.[83]

Under this scenario, as the elite became a burden to society, city economies began to crumble. Coupled with problems like famine and disease this situation caused the Maya to lose faith in their kings and consequently their civilization. Perhaps, then, the ultimate cause of the demise of the Maya civilization was a psychological crisis—a loss of belief in those qualities that drove the civilization to greatness in the first place.

The ruins of Tuluum are a symbol of a once vibrant society.

PRAYER OF A MODERN MAYA PRIEST

Many of today's Maya profess to be Christians, but their religious practices include many elements of their ancient religion. For example, George Stuart, in his book Mysterious Maya, *points out that this prayer, chanted in the Zinacantan region by Mayans who are Roman Catholic priests, honors the coming of the new year in a way reminiscent of ancient Maya ceremonies.*

These offerings are not piled high,
They are not heaped high,
It is only a small bit,
It is only a humble amount,
    But grant us thy divine pardon,
    Grant us thy divine forgiveness,
    Receive this humble spray of flowers,
    Receive this humble branch of pine,
    Receive this humble bit of incense,
    Receive this humble cloud of smoke . . . .
    Receive then: your holy sun has gone over the
      hill,
    Your holy year has passed,
    Take this for the holy end of the year,
    Take this for the holy end of the day. . . .

A modern Maya priest leads a prayer during the celebration of the Maya New Year.

The End of the World

Whatever caused the demise of the Maya civilization, one thing is certain: it brought an end to a culture that was as rich as those of ancient Greece and Rome. Michael Coe notes:

> It was not just the "stela cult"—the inscribed glorification of royal lineages and their achievements—that disappeared, but an entire world of esoteric knowledge, mythology, and ritual. Much of the elite cultural behavior . . . such as the complex Underworld mythology and iconography found on Classic Maya funerary ceramics, failed to re-emerge with the advent of the Post-Classic era, and one can only conclude that the royalty and nobility, including the scribes who were the repository of so much sacred and scientific knowledge, had "gone with the wind."[84]

Though the Maya continued to exist after the Classic period—the Golden Age of the Maya—was over, and though they subsequently survived many threats to their well-being and their culture, they never regained their former glory. Moreover, after the Spanish Conquest many were killed by their conquerors or were subjugated to them, or they succumbed to disease or became wanderers living meager existences in their former cities or their environs. And sadly, according to Michael Coe, "these dwindling groups would have known little about the glories of the Classic past."[85]

Notes

Introduction: Piecing Together a Civilization

1. George E. Stuart and Gene S. Stuart, *The Mysterious Maya*. Washington, DC: National Geographic Society, 1977, p. 40.

2. Stuart and Stuart, *The Mysterious Maya*, pp. 40 and 49.

3. Peter D. Harrison, *The Lords of Tikal: Rulers of an Ancient Maya City*. London: Thames and Hudson, 1999, p. 12.

4. Quoted in Elizabeth P. Benson, *The Maya World*. New York: Thomas Y. Crowell Company, 1967, p. 98.

Chapter 1: The Origins of Mayan Culture

5. Robert J. Sharer, *Daily Life in Maya Civilization*. Westport, CT: Greenwood Press, 1996, p. 20.

6. Michael D. Coe, *The Maya*. New York: Thames and Hudson, 1987, p. 32.

7. Linda Schele and David Freidel, *A Forest of Kings: The Untold Story of the Ancient Maya*. New York: Quill (William Morrow), 1990, p. 39.

8. Schele and Freidel, *A Forest of Kings*, p. 39.

9. Coe, *The Maya*, p. 45.

10. Coe, *The Maya*, p. 38.

11. Schele and Freidel, *A Forest of Kings*, p. 30.

12. Pamela Francis, *What Became of the Mayas?* Exeter, England: A. Wheaton & Co., 1969, p. 5.

13. Coe, *The Maya*, pp. 39–40.

14. Sylvanus G. Morley and George W. Brainerd, *The Ancient Maya*. Stanford, CA: Stanford University Press, 1983, p. 59.

15. Morley and Brainerd, *The Ancient Maya*, p. 59.

Chapter 2: Maya Society

16. Schele and Freidel, *A Forest of Kings*, p. 103.

17. Schele and Freidel, *A Forest of Kings*, pp. 97–98.

18. Morley and Brainerd, *The Ancient Maya*, p. 93.

19. Schele and Freidel, *A Forest of Kings*, pp. 94–95.

20. Quoted in Benson, *The Maya World*, p. 32.

21. Thomas Gann and J. Eric Thompson, *The History of the Maya*. London: Charles Scribner's Sons, 1931, p. 185.

22. Benson, *The Maya World*, p. 35.

23. Gann and Thompson, *The History of the Maya*, p. 36.

24. Gann and Thompson, *The History of the Maya*, p. 36.

25. Gann and Thompson, *The History of the Maya*, p. 32.

Chapter 3: Maya Ideology

26. Schele and Freidel, *A Forest of Kings*, p. 65.

27. Coe, *The Maya*, p. 164.

28. Harrison, *The Lords of Tikal: Rulers of an Ancient Maya City*, p. 59.

29. Harrison. *The Lords of Tikal: Rulers of an Ancient Maya City*, p. 60.

30. Coe, *The Maya*, p. 165.

31. Schele and Freidel, *A Forest of Kings*, p. 65.

32. Quoted in Stuart and Stuart, *The Mysterious Maya*, pp. 97–98.

33. Delia Goetz and Sylvanus G. Morley, *Popol Vuh: The Sacred Book of the Ancient Quiché Maya,* trans. Adrián Recinos. Norman, OK, and London: University of Oklahoma Press, 1991, pp. 156–59.

34. Sharer, *Daily Life in Maya Civilization,* p. 158.

35. Harrison, *The Lords of Tikal: Rulers of an Ancient Maya City,* pp. 182–83.

Chapter 4: Art and Architecture

36. Harrison, *The Lords of Tikal: Rulers of an Ancient Maya City,* p. 9.

37. Benson, *The Maya World,* p. 46.

38. Schele and Freidel, *A Forest of Kings,* pp. 103–104.

39. Gann and Thompson, *The History of the Maya,* pp. 99–100.

40. Stuart and Stuart, *The Mysterious Maya,* p. 73.

41. Schele and Freidel, *A Forest of Kings,* pp. 111–13.

42. Schele and Freidel, *A Forest of Kings,* pp. 109-10.

43. Schele and Freidel, *A Forest of Kings,* p. 111.

44. George W. Brainerd, *The Maya Civilization.* Los Angeles: Southwest Museum, 1954, pp. 58–59.

45. Stuart and Stuart, *The Mysterious Maya,* p. 75.

46. Benson, *The Maya World,* pp. 84–85.

47. Stuart and Stuart, *The Mysterious Maya,* p. 25.

48. Harrison, *The Lords of Tikal,* pp. 61–62.

49. Benson, *The Maya World,* pp. 87–89.

50. Stuart and Stuart, *The Mysterious Maya,* p. 98.

51. Stuart and Stuart, *The Mysterious Maya,* p. 76.

Chapter 5: Intellectual Pursuits

52. Morley and Brainerd, *The Ancient Maya,* p. 548.

53. Gann and Thompson, *The History of the Maya,* p. 209.

54. Morley and Brainerd, *The Ancient Maya,* p. 555.

55. Morley and Brainerd, *The Ancient Maya,* p. 555.

56. Morley and Brainerd, *The Ancient Maya,* p. 556.

57. Morley and Brainerd, *The Ancient Maya,* p. 558.

58. Morley and Brainerd, *The Ancient Maya,* p. 559.

59. Quoted in Morley and Brainerd, *The Ancient Maya,* p. 560.

60. Coe, *The Maya,* p. 176.

61. Coe, *The Maya,* p. 178.

62. Coe, *The Maya,* p. 178.

63. Benson, *The Maya World,* p. 105.

64. Coe, *The Maya,* p. 182.

65. Benson, *The Maya World,* p. 96.

66. Coe, *The Maya,* p. 180.

Chapter 6: The Decline of the Maya Civilization

67. Coe, *The Maya,* p. 126.

68. Coe, *The Maya,* p. 131.

69. Coe, *The Maya,* p. 147.

70. Coe, *The Maya,* p. 153.

71. Coe, *The Maya,* p. 153.

72. Benson, *The Maya World,* p. 125.

73. Benson, *The Maya World,* pp. 128–30.

74. Stuart and Stuart, *The Mysterious Maya,*

p. 92.

75. Stuart and Stuart, *The Mysterious Maya*, p. 92.

76. Benson, *The Maya World*, p. 127.

77. Benson, *The Maya World*, p. 128.

78. Quoted in Coe, *The Maya*, pp. 127–28.

79. Quoted in Stuart and Stuart, *The Mysterious Maya*, p. 91.

80. Benson, *The Maya World*, p. 126.

81. Quoted in Stuart and Stuart, *The Mysterious Maya*, p. 92.

82. Benson, *The Maya World*, p. 131.

83. Schele and Freidel, *A Forest of Kings*, pp. 379–80.

84. Coe, *The Maya*, p. 128.

85. Coe, *The Maya*, p. 128.

For Further Reading

Books

Leonard Everett Fisher, *Gods and Goddesses of the Ancient Maya*. New York: Holiday House, 1999. This book provides information about a dozen Maya deities.

Irene Flum Galvin and R.C. Stein, *The Ancient Maya*. New York: Benchmark Books, 1997. This book provides an overview of ancient Maya culture.

C. Bruce Hunter, *A Guide to Ancient Maya Ruins*. Norman: University of Oklahoma Press, 1986. For more advanced readers, this is a guidebook for travelers to ancient Maya ruins.

Arthur Meier Schlesinger and Fred L. Israel, eds. *Ancient Civilizations of the Aztecs and Maya: Chronicles from National Geographic*. Philadelphia: Chelsea House, 1999. This provides information from National Geo-graphic expeditions to lands of the Aztec and Maya civilizations.

Victoria Sherrow, *Maya Indians*. New York: Chelsea House, 1994. This book provides an overview of Maya culture.

Websites

Florida International University Libraries (www.fiu.edu/~library/internet/subjects/maya.html) This website provides detailed information about all aspects of Maya history, culture, and environment and lists resources where readers can acquire still more information.

Jeeni Criscenzo (www.jaguar-sun.com) This website of the author of a novel about the ancient Maya entitled *Place of Mirrors* offers many facts about ancient and modern Maya as well as links to other Maya-related sites.

Works Consulted

Elizabeth P. Benson, *The Maya World.* New York: Thomas Y. Crowell Company, 1967. This overview of ancient Maya civilization was written by an expert in pre-Columbia cultures, art, and architecture.

George W. Brainerd, *The Maya Civilization.* Los Angeles: Southwest Museum, 1954. This slim volume reports on Brainerd's exploration of Maya ruins.

Michael D. Coe, *The Maya.* New York: Thames and Hudson, 1987. Written by a professor of anthropology, this work is considered one of the most readable and authoritative accounts of the Maya civilization.

Pamela Francis, *What Became of the Mayas?* Exeter, England: A. Wheaton & Co., 1969. This book focuses on possible explanations for why the Maya deserted many of their cities in the ninth century.

Thomas Gann and J. Eric Thompson, *The History of the Maya.* London: Charles Scribner's Sons, 1931. Dr. Thomas Gann led an expedition to several Maya ruins in the 1890s; this work reports on his observations in addition to providing information on Maya history.

Delia Goetz and Sylvanus G. Morley, *Popol Vuh: The Sacred Book of the An-cient Quiché Maya.* Trans. Adrián Recinos. Norman, OK, and London: University of Oklahoma Press, 1991. This book is a translation of ancient writings by the Quiché Maya.

Peter D. Harrison, *The Lords of Tikal: Rulers of an Ancient Maya City.* London: Thames and Hudson, 1999. This book reports on Dr. Harrison's excavations of Tikal ruins during the 1950s and 1960s.

Sylvanus G. Morley and George W. Brainerd, *The Ancient Maya.* Stanford, CA: Stanford University Press, 1983. This complex scholarly work provides detailed information on all aspects of ancient Maya civilization.

Linda Schele and David Freidel, *A Forest of Kings: The Untold Story of the Ancient Maya.* New York: Quill (William Morrow), 1990. Written by two of the foremost experts on the ancient Maya, this work provides fanciful descriptions of what life was like among the ancient Maya as well as scholarly information about archaeological findings related to ancient Maya ruins.

Robert J. Sharer, *Daily Life in Maya Civilization.* Westport, CT: Greenwood Press, 1996. Professor Robert Sharer is an expert on Maya culture, and his work is one of the best on daily life among the ancient Maya.

George E. Stuart and Gene S. Stuart, *The Mysterious Maya*. Washington, DC: National Geographic Society, 1977. This book reports on the condition of the Maya people today, comparing their present situation to their past.

Index

Picture Credits

Cover Photo: © Charles and Josette Lenars/CORBIS

© AFP/CORBIS, 45

© Archivo Iconografico, S.A./CORBIS, 38

© Richard A. Cooke/CORBIS, 71

© Sergio Dorantes/CORBIS, 73

© Macduff Everton/CORBIS, 31, 37

© Arvind Garg/CORBIS, 41, 65

© Danny Lehman/CORBIS, 11, 49, 55, 64

© Charles & Josette Lenars/CORBIS, 83, 98

North Wind Picture Archives, 9, 26, 51, 60, 80

© Gianni Dagli Orti/CORBIS, 33, 90, 96

© Reuters NewMedia Inc./CORBIS, 93, 99

Courtesy of Amy Santos, 62

© Michael T. Sedam/CORBIS, 56

© Roman Soumer/CORBIS, 19

Stock Montage, 76, 87

© Francisco Venturi/CORBIS, 16, 21, 69

About the Author

Patricia D. Netzley is the author of dozens of books for children, young adults, and adults. Her nonfiction books include *The Stone Age, The Encyclopedia of Environmental Literature, The Curse of King Tut, Haunted Houses, Life on a Mt. Everest Expedition, The Encyclopedia of Women's Travel and Exploration, The Encyclopedia of Movie Special Effects, The Encyclopedia of Witchcraft,* and *The Encyclopedia of Ancient Egypt.*